Whispers
from Our
Soul

Whispers
from Our
Soul

The Voice of Tahkamenon

Valerie Wilkinson
Russell Reed

HAMPTON ROADS
PUBLISHING COMPANY, INC.
for the evolving human spirit

Cover design by Mayapriya Long

For information write:

Hampton Roads Publishing Company, Inc.
134 Burgess Lane
Charlottesville, VA 22902

Or call: 804-296-2772
FAX: 804-296-5096
e-mail: hrpc@hrpub.com
Web site: http://www.hrpub.com

If you are unable to order this book from your local
bookseller, you may order directly from the publisher.
Quantity discounts for organizations are available.
Call 1-800-766-8009, toll-free.

Library of Congress Catalog Card Number: 99-71619
ISBN 1-57174-138-0
10 9 8 7 6 5 4 3 2 1

Printed on acid-free recycled paper in Canada

Dedication

For my husband Brian.
Your beauty and authenticity
have captured my heart and changed my life.
Thank you for sharing your soul.

—Valerie

For those who have loved me for my heart and
chosen not to pay too much attention to the rest.
Thanks to Val and T for sharing.
To my mom and dad for teaching me that love,
no matter what, does come first.
To Peter and Autumn, for choosing me for their
dad.
I thank, love, and worship you.
To Mary Ellen, my bride and my lover, thanks for
seeing my beauty and having the courage to
show me the way to my soul.
And to all my Sheehy family—love, love, love.

—Russ

With a special dedication to
Ken Wilkinson
who taught us of love's significance with his life
and of its permanence with his death.

Acknowledgments

We gratefully acknowledge all those who
encouraged, supported, and inspired us
throughout this journey.

Our heartfelt thanks to:

❖ Tahkamenon, for sharing his wisdom and opening our hearts,

❖ Brian and Mary Ellen, for their unfailing support,

❖ Ashleigh, Eric, Alex, Peter, and Autumn, for their unfailing optimism,

❖ Our friends, extended families, and coworkers, for their enthusiasm and patience,

❖ Russ's staff members, for their continual support,

❖ Ted Scallet, for his insightful legal advice,

❖ Cid Scallet and Cindy Dorney, for their belief in the writing and the importance of the message,

❖ Jill Smolowe, for her expert editorial advice,

❖ Doug MacKinnon, for way more than his share of patience, encouragement, and guidance,

❖ Richard Fleder, for his compassion and support,

❖ Our publisher, Bob Friedman, for his integrity, insight, and commitment,

❖ Joe Dunn, for recognizing our potential,

❖ Ruth O'Lill Dunn, for recognizing our fear,

❖ The regulators, for bringing the two of us together,

❖ Eddie Garcia, for teaching us that courage is not about a moment, but a way that we choose to live our lives,

❖ And finally, to our souls, which are now such a distinct and important part of our daily existence that we feel the need to thank them specifically.

Our connection is all the stronger for the love that
each of you has brought into our lives.

Listen while I whisper
All the secrets
Of your soul.
Fall within my rhythm.
Find the beat
That makes you
Whole.
Listen.
Won't you listen?
Feed the hunger
Of your heart.
You are but an actor
Caught up playing
Many parts.
Listen to my story,
To my ancient,
Sacred song.
Find yourself a moment.
Come on back
Where you belong.

—Tahkamenon

Part One

❖

The Discovery

Chapter One

I never considered entertaining spirits nor, for that matter, being entertained by them.

My only thoughts of the afterlife were of teenage seances, ouija board predictions, and one dubious meeting with a fortune-teller. That is why I found all I am about to relate so surprising; frightening at times, comforting at others. I will do my best to allow for your skepticism just as I learned to allow for my own.

For many months, I doubted the voice, the occurrences, the message. It was all so removed from anything I had ever before believed. I had thought myself open-minded. Although I did not exactly believe in spirits, it was mostly a passive decision. I thought little of my own conviction and had no particular disdain for those who claimed connections with the afterlife. I did question their sincerity when they used their supposed connection for profit or manipulation. Still, I could not deny my curiosity when I heard that a psychic had helped solve a crime or had related a vision that later proved to be true.

Such was my state of mind about these things when I was visited one night by my father-in-law, Ken. He came to talk about Brian, my husband, his son, to tell me of his pride at Brian's accomplishments and his belief in our future. He said many beautiful and comforting things. Were it not for the fact that he had died over a year and a half earlier, I would have enjoyed the conversation thoroughly.

As it was, I was terrified. Or more exactly, alternating between terror, disbelief, and joy. I do not know how long the encounter lasted. Time, it seems, is a relative and imprecise measurement when applied to spiritual matters.

Ken had come to me in the bed I shared with Brian. As I stared ahead at the outline of my husband peacefully curled up in my arms, Ken's indentation on the water bed behind me was undeniable. I wanted to turn and look, but my fear of what I might see and of silencing the beautiful voice kept me frozen in my place.

Ken talked steadily, describing his pride in Brian as a husband and a father, his delight as he watched his son with his grandchildren, his pride in our relationship and in our willingness to sacrifice for each other's dreams. He spoke of Brian's job, of the rocky path that we had taken to find it, of his certainty that Brian would finally be happy with his work. He talked mostly of love and reassurance, ending it all with an emphatic declaration that no matter the obstacles, we would always be okay.

A beautiful flow of words and then silence. I held still for a very long time, afraid to turn, wanting the voice to continue, wishing to ask questions I had not thought of while he was speaking. Until the quiet which followed his voice, I had only listened, my mind racing at the incredu-lity of this moment, my heart rejoicing at the beauty of this spiritual embrace.

It seemed like hours before I no longer felt the presence on the bed and still longer before I summoned the courage to roll over and face the spot where Ken had lain. I desper-ately had to go to the bathroom but was afraid at every step that I would see an apparition. Although my eyes had adjusted fully to the darkness, I turned the light on in the bathroom and quietly shut the door.

I sat for a long time, rubbing my temples and replaying what I could of the words over and over again in my mind. Already I was losing some of the specifics, but the overall message and gentle tone of Ken's voice remained. I tried to convince myself that I had been dreaming, but I knew absolutely that that was untrue. I had been completely awake. Nothing of the event had unfolded as a dream. There was no filter, no fuzziness, no disjointedness in his speech. Every statement logically followed the other with no interposing people or ideas to break the sequence. It all ended naturally as if he clearly had said all that he had come to say. There was no waking up when it was over, only staring at the outline of my husband in the darkness.

As I turned off the light and stumbled back to my bed, I thought solely of Brian. "Should I wake him? Should I tell him? Why did his father choose to speak to me and not to him?" Brian slept on, totally unaffected by all that had just transpired. I immediately worried that he would be upset by my description of the encounter, that he might feel left out or think that I had finally crossed the fine line on the edge of sanity. I decided not to wake him, to put off at least until morning the need to explain the unexplainable.

It was now 4:00 a.m. I had two more hours until the alarm. I spent them fitfully, drifting in and out of sleep. My adrenaline levels kept me far from anything that resembled rest. I closed my eyes, still fighting off moments of fear. The disbelief would wash over me and then subside. There was no doubt when I replayed the encounter for myself. Doubt entered only when I thought of describing the situation to Brian. Or to anyone else.

I jumped at the blare of the alarm and quickly reached over to slide the lever to off. My husband continued sleeping at my side. Much more gently than usual, I reached over to rub his back and softly coax him from his sleep. I felt protective, almost maternal. I was afraid of rocking his world and dredging up his grief. I too had suffered through the loss of my father, only five years earlier. I was not convinced that Brian had dealt with all of the emotions of losing a parent. It is a delicate process. I feared this news might be an unwelcome and potentially harmful jolt.

He woke as usual with a sparkling smile. "Good morning beautiful."

I leaned over and kissed him, overcome by emotion, not yet trusting myself to speak.

He noticed nothing different and hugged me briefly before getting out of bed. "Rough schedule today?" he asked, as he gathered his clothes and headed toward the shower.

"You know, just the usual," I replied, relieved when he shut the bathroom door. Instead of immediately starting my rounds to rouse our three young children, pick out clothes for the day, help them get dressed, and place them in front of cartoons so that I too could get ready, I lay in bed staring at the ceiling, everything seeming so different with the light filtering in through the curtains.

I resolved not to tell Brian now. It would be too rushed. Mornings were always crazy with three kids and two careers. Throwing in my highlights of last night's appearance of his dead father would make it impossible to get out of the door on time. It would not be fair to tell him without an opportunity to digest the story. Besides I was still considering not telling him at all. Against everything I typically believed about honesty and relationships, I had to wonder if this were not one of those rare secrets better kept to myself.

I still could not quite accept all that had happened. Luckily, I had no idea of what lay ahead. Had I known at that time, I probably would not have had the strength that morning to pull myself from my bed.

From that point on, the morning passed in a blur. I am certain that I dressed, fed, and carted our children off to their respective schools. I am sure that I counted out lunch money, had two cups of coffee, and kissed Brian good-bye. This was our weekly morning routine. It always was rushed but rarely required much independent thought.

Once alone in the van, I turned on the radio. I had not bothered to turn it on until Ashleigh, Eric, and Alex had all been dropped off at their schools. The radio only made them yell louder as they reminded me of upcoming field trips and science projects due, asked if I remembered to pack their library books, and said to me that, of course, "You did pack enough lunch money for ice cream, didn't you?" As the door shut behind the last child, I instinctively pressed the radio knob. The van filled with the mellow sounds of the easy listening channel that I detested for the compromise of my youth it represented, but that I accepted as the most that I could handle between the chaos of my morning and the chaos of my job. Unfortunately, today even Billy Joel overwhelmed me, my mind bursting with conflicting and convergent thoughts. I pressed the knob again and heard only the sounds of the wind and the road.

"This cannot be happening to me," I thought again and again. "I am a CPA, for God's sake. Three kids, one husband.

I drive a minivan. I run a multimillion-dollar corporation. Me? Me? How can I have had a late night chat with a dead person?"

In addition to the endless questioning, the previous night's discussion itself ran over and over in the back of my mind, complete with the emotions of the moment, the feeling of the indentation behind me on the water bed, the outline of Brian's sleeping body in the darkness in front. I felt disbelief but only at the concept. Ken was dead; therefore he could not have been in my bedroom last night, speaking to me. But he was there. I was certain of that. My skepticism shattered as I allowed the specifics to rise to the surface, as I remembered my fear and his gentleness. I could not disbelieve this had happened even as I could not accept that it was possible.

This was my torment as I arrived at my office, determined to push these thoughts from my mind and focus on the business of the day. Luckily, at least for the moment, my job was consuming, both intellectually and emotionally. I was in charge of a growing company that offered health-care coverage to thousands of participants in several states across the country. Currently we were at war with both federal and state governments over the proper regulation and jurisdiction of our health-care plan. We had initiated several lawsuits against the various governmental entities. They, in turn, were threatening to shut us down at any moment or certainly at any false step. In addition to fighting the legal battle, I was leading a legislative initiative to clarify the law and prohibit future stonewalling by the federal government.

Of course, there was also an office to run, supplies to run out of, schedules to coordinate, temperaments to conflict, and always at least one participant angry over some aspect of the plan provisions. This made it easy to find a crisis and to overcome the torment of the previous eight hours. All I had to do was choose which crisis to deal with first.

Checking my calendar for the day, I realized that the majority of the morning was blocked off for a conference call with our claims administrator. We were trying to finalize the terms of our service contract. As is often the case in business, they had been handling our medical claims for close to a year, but we still had not agreed to the specific wording of the contract. It would be another morning of reviewing every word and omission, turning each on its side and then back again, trying to glean every possible interpretation, discussing the issues as if among friends, each knowing that the other was trying to gain the advantage should the contract ever be pulled forward in the scrutiny of litigation.

It was a tedious job, but I hoped it somehow would be compelling enough to keep my mind on track. Fortunately, Russ Reed was a necessary part of the conversation. Russ was our insurance consultant. He had helped find the claims administrator as well as a reinsurer to carry excess risk for our health-care plan. He had done this when we were small, with no track record, and with little to recommend us other than the character and integrity of the people involved with the deal.

Russ believed in us from the start, and he used his extensive contacts in the insurance industry to build relationships for us. As a result of the swirling intrigue and innuendo surrounding our regulatory battle with the government, one such relationship blew up shortly after it commenced. Most people in the industry viewed our plan as too hot to handle. Not Russ. He worked even harder, replacing the failed contract with another, giving viability and credibility to our plan as I worked to keep it going from both the operational and legal perspectives.

Through the intensity of the battle, Russ and I developed a business relationship and friendship much deeper than our two years of acquaintance as consultant and client typically would have entailed. He lived in Philadelphia, I in Virginia Beach. We saw each other only once every other month or so. In fact, we had worked together for over six months before we actually met.

In spite of the distance, the relationship was significant. Because of our noticeable attachment, many of our co-workers suspected an affair. They were wrong. While there was a strong attraction, it was not sexual. Russ and I were both happily married. This relationship was special, different; the attraction was not physical but strong enough to confuse us both.

I was glad that this morning would be spent on the phone with Russ, even if it did mean that we would have to discuss the definition of "termination" for the eighteenth time. The conference call went forth much as I had expected. Russ and I on one side fighting for our interpretations, two others from the claims administrator carefully representing their own interests. I stayed attentive through the crucial points, making sure to get in all of the specific comments and questions I had noted on my draft of the contract. When the conversation was overtaken by obscure "what if" scenarios ("What if the computer, the back up, and the tapes all fail at once? What if each participant across the country decides to call at the same time?"), I allowed myself to wander back to the events of the previous night.

As I once again relived the encounter, I wanted to tell Russ what had transpired the night before. The idea started slowly, seeping into my consciousness instead of rushing right in. "Wait. This does not make any sense," I thought. "Why would I tell Russ something that I'm not even sure I can trust to my husband?" But the fact that Russ was not my husband was part of the draw. He may think I was crazy, but he could not be hurt in any way by the disclosure, as I still feared Brian might. I thought also of my reputation. This was our insurance consultant. We depended on each other a great deal in business. Given the intensity of the battle that surrounded this company on so many fronts, I could not afford to alienate my allies. Russ thought I was intelligent, honest, shrewd. He considered me an asset in any meeting or discussion regarding our plan. What would he think if I suddenly told him that I slept with ghosts? No, it was too great a risk. No matter the strength of our friendship, I could not tell him this.

The conference call continued for another half hour before everyone agreed it was enough "legalese" for one day. We would write up the changes, pass them by both sets of lawyers, and get together again to go over the next round of questions that these changes inevitably would create.

As we were getting off the phone, all parties making small talk and inquiring as to the families, loved ones, and favorite athletic teams of the others, I recalled something that Russ had told me long ago. We had been talking one Monday morning about the previous weekend. This was pretty standard—"Just great, two soccer games and karate. How was yours?"—when Russ added something that I thought strange at the time. He said that the weekend had been the usual—running errands, playing with his daughter Autumn, trying to find some quiet time with his wife, Mary Ellen. Then he added, "Mary Ellen's sister came over on Sunday, and they talked for hours about channeling angels."

I was only vaguely familiar with the term "channeling." I was not certain whether Russ was kidding or not. His tone was complacent, no hint of humor or sarcasm. I found the statement odd and was unsure how to respond, so I said nothing. It soon was forgotten amid talk of contracts, reinsurance, and lawsuits. And it had stayed forgotten until now.

The others disconnected from the call. "Russ, I've got to ask your advice about something," I blurted, surprising even myself.

"What? Yeah, yeah, okay. Hello. Hello. Are you sure they're off the phone? I never trust these things."

"Yes. I'm sure," I responded, fearful that I would lose my nerve if I did not move fast. "They're off. I can tell by the lights. Listen. You're not going to believe what happened to me last night."

"Okay. What? What?"

"Brian's father came and talked to me." Russ had heard all of the ups and downs as Brian and I had dealt with his father's diagnosis of cancer and his relatively swift death. Therefore there was no need to add, "Oh yeah, and by the way, he was dead when we had this conversation."

"Cool," came the immediate reply. "What did he say?"

"Cool. What do you mean cool? I'm telling you that I talked to a dead person last night and you say 'cool'?"

"Val, this is Russell. Believe me, everyone I know talks to dead people. What did he say?"

"Russ, you are so bizarre. Don't make fun of me." The agitation that often accompanied our conversations was starting to rise.

"I'm not. I'm serious. Tell me what he said."

I was confused by Russ's reaction but determined to share my story with him and ask his advice on telling Brian. I related the proceedings as best I could, describing the clarity of Ken's voice, the outline of Brian's body, the movement on the water bed, the fear and the comfort of

Ken's presence. I told Russ all I could remember—Ken's pride for Brian's accomplishments and his assurances for our future and our happiness. When I finally fell quiet, Russ jumped right in.

"Christ, what did Brian say?"

"I haven't told him."

"You haven't told him? You've got to tell him. Why wouldn't you? How wonderful. His dad just wanted to say he loved him and that he will be all right. Of course you've got to tell him. Tonight."

"What if he thinks I'm crazy?" My question was serious, tormented, heartfelt.

Russ laughed. "Crazy. Brian think you're crazy? That's what you are afraid of?" More laughter although I failed to get his joke. "This man has lived with you for how long? And you think he's just now figuring out that you're crazy? Hell Valerie, give him some credit would you."

Russ said this with such benevolence that I had to laugh in spite of my irritation. He was right of course. In comparison with the balance of my life with Brian, this would probably seem no more insane than any of the millions of other moments that we had either shared or discussed over the years. So far he had continued to love me. I guessed passing along his father's love and assurances was certainly worth the risk.

Later that night, after dinner, baths, and bedtime for our children, Brian and I curled up together on the couch. I told him of his father's visit. I related the comforting words as vividly and as accurately as I could. Much to my amazement, he never questioned it happening, never even suggested that I must have been dreaming. When I finished talking, he lay silent for a long time, stretched out on the sofa, his head in my lap. After several minutes, I felt tears running along my fingers. Their dampness surprised me, as there was no accompanying noise, no sniffles, no gentle shaking of his body, no deepness to his breath.

"Are you happy or sad?" I asked.

"Both," he replied, sitting up to hold me in his arms.

"Me too. It really was special." I closed my eyes for a moment, thinking of Ken. "He really was special."

"Why do you think he spoke to you and not to me?" Brian asked.

"I'm not sure. Maybe he knew I would hear him." I drew back a little and smiled at my husband. "Maybe he knows how soundly you sleep and didn't figure that he stood a chance." Brian smiled back. "I'm certain from what he said that the message was mainly for you. He loves you very, very much."

We were both choked with emotion. "I miss him," Brian said, the words catching in his throat. "At certain times. Like with the children. Do you think he'll come back?"

"I don't know what to think," I replied, "except I'm fairly certain that he never really left."

The truth was that I had no idea if he would return or what would happen next. And even if I had ventured to guess at that moment, I would never have imagined the incredible spiritual journey upon which I was about to embark.

Chapter Two

Russ called the next morning almost as soon as I arrived at my desk, unusual for someone who has an aversion to mornings and who luckily works for himself so that he can adjust his schedule accordingly. "Did you tell him?"

"Don't you ever say 'hello'?"

"Hello. Did you tell him?"

"Yes, but you are being rude, so I'm not going to tell you what he said."

Russ laughed on the other end of the line. "So he thinks you're crazy."

"You jerk. What was this all, a set-up? 'Oh, go ahead and tell him. You have to tell him,'" I said, mimicking his advice from the day before. "You were just hoping that he would think I was crazy. Well, he didn't, and I'm not. And that just goes to show you why I am so happily married to this man."

"Okay. Okay. Maybe he is just blinded enough by love

not to realize what a true wacko you are. Fortunately, I'm more objective." Russ paused for a moment, shifting gears. "But seriously, what did he say?"

"Very little. It was so emotional. He wondered why Ken had spoken to me and not to him. He asked if I thought his father would come back. I don't know. I didn't really consider it until he asked."

"Maybe he will," Russ replied thoughtfully. "Don't know."

"Anyway, thanks for listening yesterday. I felt as if my mind was going to explode."

"Yuck. That would be messy. But it was no problem. I've been talking to spirits since I was a child, so this is really no big deal."

"You're always trying to provoke me. Stop saying crazy things."

"It's not crazy. I have. I even write down some of my conversations." There was brief pause. I was at a loss for an appropriate response. "See, now you think I'm the one who is crazy."

"Think?"

"Very funny." Russ sounded more serious than before. "I've been meaning to talk with you about this anyway. Maybe you could help me with the writing."

I struggled to follow Russ's line of thinking. "Writing what? What are you talking about?"

"My conversations with spirits. Well, one spirit really—Tahkamenon."

"Talka who?" I asked, feeling irritated and not knowing why.

"Tahkamenon. The Big T."

"Okay," I thought to myself, "This man not only has an imaginary friend but he has given him an impossible name and a stupid nickname. I really must choose my friends more wisely."

"He says the most incredible things," Russ continued. "I've tried to write some of them down over the years. But it's hard. When he speaks, it's so profound and so specific. As soon as I try to repeat it, either to myself or on paper, I'm just left with the essence. It's hard to capture the words."

I remembered sitting in the bathroom just two nights before, trying to replicate Ken's words but feeling successful only as to the overall content, surprising since I have a knack for remembering important conversations verbatim, often for months, sometimes for years. "Will you send it to me?"

"What?" Russ asked.

"What you've written."

"Yes. No. I don't know." I sensed panic in Russ's voice. "Not yet. It wouldn't make much sense to you. It's just snippets really. Let me try to get more down. Maybe you can do that magic thing you do with words. You've always wanted to write a book. We could write a book together."

"Yeah sure," I responded laughing. "Insurance salesman talks to the Big T as translated by health-care administrator and CPA. Sounds like a winner to me. They'll be breaking down the doors."

"Do I sense a degree of sarcasm?"

"Ah, you really do have ESP!"

"Forget it then. I'm not sending you anything."

"No please. I'm only kidding. Well I'm not sure about a book, but I truly want to read what you have written. What an intriguing side of you I've never known."

"That's me. Mysterious and intriguing. Not to mention incredibly charming and handsome."

"I'll be sure to put that in the book. You know not everyone is as perceptive as you are. There may just be a person or two who does not pick up on all of your qualities on their own."

Good thing I didn't hold my breath waiting for the writing. Even though Russ had been amazed at my reluctance to share the details of the encounter with my father-in-law, he let months pass before sharing with me any real details of his conversations with Tahkamenon.

Thanks to my persistence, I did learn a little here and there. I could neither remember nor pronounce the name Tahkamenon (pronounced Talk-a-men-on) so we typically stuck with "The Big T" or simply "T." Russ related stories of conversations with T that reached all the way back to his childhood. T had been there as a friend to this only child, as comfort in the jungles of Vietnam, as guidance during the pitfalls of his first marriage and divorce, and as assurance during his estrangement from his son, Peter, that haunted him still.

He told me of the discussions but little about them. Russ claimed that what T spoke of was much greater than his individual experience. According to Russ, T spoke of the world and humanity and of the ability of each of us to listen with our souls. T did not give Russ detailed guidance as often as he inspired him to hope, to love, to believe. That was about as specific as Russ would get, but even with this little bit of information, I was certain that these conversations had had a profound impact on his life.

I wanted more than ever to read what Russ had written, but he always had an excuse. "I can't find the pages. I've found the pages, but they need to be typed. My secretary is busy, and it will take me forever to type them. They are typed but need to be proofread. I'm too swamped but will get to it as soon as I return from vacation. The fax machine is broken. What do you mean? I'm not making excuses!"

Two months passed. My conversation with my father-in-law was now a treasured memory, a special gift that I was glad to have received. Nothing further had happened, but I was much more open to the thought of communicating with spirits, more attentive to the presence of my soul.

I was curious about Russ, both about his talks with Tahkamenon and about his reluctance to open up about them. Here was a man who had served as top management of the Hartford Insurance Company, a former New York City insurance guy who had owned a Ferrari and a large home with an indoor pool. This was a man who thrived on networking, on deal-making, on profit. This was not the type of person who I would have imagined talked with spirits, especially routinely, and even had them talk back.

Finally Russ gave a little, a sketchy rundown of topics he and T had discussed. As I happened to be sitting at my desk and it was very much my habit, I took notes as he spoke.

- ❖ Religion is with purpose, without rules.
- ❖ What has man created? It is all just rearrangement.
- ❖ Harnessing of light/harnessing of energy.
- ❖ Environmentalists—three-year-olds taking care of mother.
- ❖ Ability is only to destroy planet, not souls.
- ❖ Convergent paths.
- ❖ +/-, yin/yang, good/bad.
- ❖ Two sides of a coin.
- ❖ 13 - 7 = 6.

So now I had this mysterious list. Interesting, but still no writing. Still no answers. I kept thinking about the book Russ had proposed. Without knowing what had transpired, without understanding anything that he had just said, I could not stop myself from believing that these conversations not only had changed Russ's life but somehow they were about to change mine as well.

That following weekend, with only the encouragement of the list, I sat down at my computer and began to write. I had no idea where I was going, what it was I intended to say. I vaguely understood that I would write about Tahkamenon but refused to think of this too seriously.

There was a sentence that haunted me. It played again and again in my mind like some old commercial jingle that refuses to budge. "From far beyond the darkness, he speaks with the power of the light." It must refer to Tahkamenon. No other explanation came to mind. So I agreed to give, to sit down at my computer, and to see just where this sentence would lead.

With chills raking my body on that August afternoon, I wrote:

From far beyond the darkness, he speaks with the power of the light. Tugging at the corners of my consciousness until I recognize his presence with absolute certainty. Speaking directly from his soul, he has no need for the fragility of form. In these moments, I do not so much see as believe, not so much listen as understand.

My thoughts flow before me with newfound clarity. He has entered the twisted chambers of my mind, littered with years of dust and debris, slowly proceeding through the maze, uncovering treasures long forgotten. He touches them almost randomly, polishing each until it gleams with the brightness of an expertly cut jewel. I sometimes wonder if he has brought the treasures to plant along the way, but I know them to be mine. Even the spaces are of my own making; yet the passage is much older and much deeper than I currently comprehend.

The maze of corridors and rooms seems strangely familiar; yet, I cannot remember what lay ahead. I turn each corner with anticipation, the view springing from my memory, past and present occurring simultaneously in my mind.

Often he is patient, handing me a jewel, half covered with dust, and watches with amusement as I eagerly rub the stone, holding it up to the light and rejoicing in the prisms of color reflecting back upon my face. Invigorating moments when I catch glimpses of myself in the reflection, pure of substance not of form. There is much work to be done. Much to discover. I cannot rest in his presence but race wildly at times from room to room, hallway to hallway. At others I am quiet, willing to remain in one room, even one space, until I have fully taken in the view.

In return for my searching, he brings me to moments of clarity, accompanied by perfect color and perfect tone. Like twisting the dials on an old television until the picture crisply leaps forward and the static vanishes from the voices. No distractions. No haze. Perfect unity.

Of course there are times when I think that he has lost the way, as I stumble deeper and deeper through mazes of hallway, his presence dimming against the impending darkness of my fear. He leads me gently at first and then pulls me forward through these moments, even as I plant my feet firmly against the ground. Occasionally my fear overtakes him—leaping from the shadows and squelching his light.

There are times when I reach for him in the daylight, but he remains beyond my grasp. And so I wonder if he truly exists or if I am suffering from some recurrent dream. Doubts that can fester and keep him away night after night until he again enters my consciousness with such impact and authenticity that it is no longer him that I doubt, but the daylight, and the fear that blocked his entrance.

I cannot recall when first I recognized his presence or the significance of his name. Tahkamenon is part of my distant memories. And while I knew him as a child, there have been stretches of time when I felt that he had abandoned me. Or even worse, that I somehow had abandoned him.

I have come to trust Tahkamenon. He will return when the fear subsides. Sometimes by my conscious willing, sometimes without. And the journey resumes until eventually we find the place he knew existed and I struggled so hard to find—the thoughts that lay hidden, far beyond the darkness, on the other side of fear.

On these pages, I will try to capture the essence of our exchanges over the years and the impact they have had upon my life. It is my sincere desire to reduce these moments into words without clouding their clarity or diminishing their meaning.

Tahkamenon is as much a part of me as he is distinct. I have no knowledge from where he comes or to where he goes. Yet I believe with all of my being that if I can capture him with my words, you will see his reflection within yourself.

When I finished, I could not believe what I had written. Not the words themselves, but the description of something I had never experienced. The description I thought immediately to be of Russ's experience. But how could this be? He had never indicated any of the details that I now told. And more than this, I was overwhelmed by the incredible feeling that overcame me. All I could think to describe it was "connected." That didn't mean much, but it was the only word that would do. Connected to what or to whom? I had no idea. But I had to show this to Russ. I called him immediately. He was home. "Don't move." I rushed to my office and faxed him the words.

The phone rang just as I returned home. I picked it up before the answering machine kicked in. "Hello," I said, a little out of breath.

"Hello." And then nothing.

"Russ, are you there?"

"Yeah." More silence.

"Russ, what is wrong with you?" I had no idea what he was doing. I usually understood his words, his nuances, even his expressions, but his silence had me stumped. "Are you going to say anything, or did you call *not* to talk to me?"

"Unbelievable." Another pause.

"Good unbelievable or bad unbelievable?"

"Unbelievable unbelievable."

"Why are you tormenting me?" I was angry with myself for faxing him the passage. This was not fair. It made me vulnerable. Now I cared too much what he thought to just give up on this ridiculous conversation and get off of the phone.

"I had no idea," Russ replied quietly.

"What? That you were tormenting me? Well most people actually talk once they—"

"No, that you were talking with Tahkamenon."

Now I was really angry. "I'm not talking to him. He's talking to you," I said, sounding like a young child fighting for attention from a mutual friend. "I only wrote what I thought it might be like."

"Exactly what it is like."

"So you like it?"

31

"Unbelievable."

This conversation was really starting to irritate me. I had never spoken to Tahkamenon. I still had difficulty saying his name. I accepted his relationship with Russ. I allowed myself to believe it possible thanks mostly to that fateful encounter with my father-in-law. But this was ridiculous. Truly. Obviously I would know if I were talking with a spirit. Another round of chills crawled up my spine and cascaded down my arms to my fingertips. That irritated me even more.

"Look, Russ, I'm glad you like it, but it is all about you. Not me. I just imagined what it must be like. That's all. Okay?"

"Yeah sure. Whatever you say," Russ replied much too easily. "Look I'm going to send you my writing this week."

"Oh, yeah. I wonder how many times I have heard that before."

"I mean it. I'm out of the office tomorrow and Tuesday, but I'll fax it on Wednesday. I promise."

I almost believed him. He had never been so specific about the time frame. Maybe sharing my writing had put him at ease. But I would not fully believe him until I held his writing in my hands.

I shared both the writing and Russ's reaction with Brian. "What's the significance of his name?" Brian asked.

"I have no idea."

"Does Russ?"

"I don't think so."

"Oh," Brian said, looking bewildered. "Well then, why did you write it?"

"I don't know," I replied. "I don't know why I wrote any of it."

Brian sighed and turned his attention back to the newspaper.

"Well?" I asked, trying to hold my irritation in check. "What do you think?"

"It's great, hon," he responded without looking up. "Really nice."

"Great, huh?" I thought to myself. "Yeah, I can see that you're touched." Still, I didn't push the issue. "Anyway it's not great," I thought. "It's unbelievable." I laughed as Russ's word came rushing into my thoughts.

"What's so funny?" Brian asked, peeking over the edge of the paper.

"Oh nothing," I answered, wondering how I would feel if Brian suddenly discovered a strong connection with someone other than me.

As I showered for work the next morning, I kept thinking about Russ's accusation that I was writing about my own encounter. It bothered me that he had sounded so unconvinced by my denial. Who the hell was he to suppose what was going on in my mind?

But then who the hell was I to so accurately describe what was going on in his?

Chapter Three

I returned again and again to the mysterious passage. I marveled at the words. I wondered at their production. Almost accidental in their creation, they lay before me now as a cohesive, comprehensive whole. I found strange comfort in the words, relishing the description of discovery, feeling the pain of moments without Tahkamenon, the relief at his return.

"What does this mean?" I thought, asking the question while resisting the answer. Scanning the pages, I was particularly drawn to the ending—"if I can capture him with my words, you will see his reflection within yourself." It seemed a call to action. "Whose words?" I wondered. "Tahkamenon's? Russ's? Mine?"

I called Russ's office while he was out of town. Mary Ellen answered. "Russ showed me your writing," she said. I took a deep breath, concerned about her reaction to both the writing and the relationship. She quickly alleviated my fears. "It's beautiful. Russ says that it is exactly what he feels."

"Thank you," I replied. "But the whole thing is very confusing."

"Well you're obviously sharing a special messenger," she responded. Unlike Brian, Mary Ellen seemed to grasp the connection that the passage drew between Russ, Tahkamenon, and myself. She stated it without question, and I found myself going forward without challenging her assumption.

"But Mary Ellen," I continued, "we're two business people. Why do you think this is happening to us? Why not to someone who is out there looking?"

"Oh, I don't know," she said thoughtfully. "Maybe you are looking. Or maybe because you are focused on business. It's an interesting perspective—if you two can talk to spirits, then why not anyone?"

"I'll try to take that as a compliment," I responded, laughing at the abruptness of her statement.

Mary Ellen laughed as well. "It was intended as one," she said and then fell quiet. "I've always known that Russ was special." Her voice sounded far away. "That he was meant for a larger purpose."

I took her words in slowly, absorbing their meaning. In many ways Russ was larger than life, his ups and downs often ricocheting off the boundaries of normal human existence. I listened intently as Mary Ellen spoke of Russ, not as a husband, but as an entity, as a force. "People are drawn to him," she continued. "His energy is just so intense."

It was interesting to see Russ briefly through her eyes. I too was drawn to his specialness. His humor was infectious. And he delighted everyone with spontaneous and infatuating stories, playing out the role of each participant with a different voice and a unique set of expressions.

As Mary Ellen spoke, I saw Russ in a different, more

meaningful, light. But even more than that, her words touched me for the easy acceptance of something I viewed as foreign and surreal. She believed effortlessly in a purpose that I could not quite grasp. I thanked her again for her kindness. She certainly seemed okay with the situation. Now, if I could just make it okay within myself.

I valued my relationship with Russ and worried about the inevitable changes that this connection would bring. Often he was the only bright spot in a day filled with contracts and lawyers. I needed our relationship desperately, much more than I had realized. I could not help but fear a loss of what we now held.

As I struggled to reconcile the connection, I noticed a growing sense of apprehension. The words were beautiful, and Russ had described his relationship with Tahkamenon with sincere love and admiration. So why was I resisting? Was it the connection itself or the responsibility that I sensed within the writing?

"To capture the words," I thought. "To allow you to see 'his reflection within yourself.'" I did not know precisely to whom the words applied. It was a problem that I would continue to wrestle with as the writing poured from the recesses of my soul. I, you, we—all confused and intermingled. None quite fitting the undefined boundaries of this newly formed, or newly recognized, partnership.

Regardless of my confusion, the sense of responsibility was clear. And I had the unfortunate habit of accepting responsibility whenever it presented itself. In many ways, it had served me well, driving me forward in my life and my career. But it also weighed me down. Given my current battle with the government, I was already overwhelmed with obligations and drowning in the expectations of others.

Fearing the answers as much as the questions, I still was driven to write. Unable to fight the desire, I resolved to reduce to paper the swirl of thoughts I could neither catch nor extinguish. I would write them. But that was all. Just the words. I was going no further. Of that much, I was perfectly clear.

My next attempt at writing was frustrated by my own apprehension, the words held at bay by my fear. Finally, I focused again on Tahkamenon, allowing the words to form themselves on the page. They flowed as they had before, with no forethought as to their design, organization, or eventual destination.

It is painful to describe the times without Tahkamenon. These are the moments that live on in my memory without color. Not even black or white. Just endless shades of gray. My thoughts and emotions void of distinction—existence unignited by passion or hope.

I have been without Tahkamenon for so long now that I struggle to remember the quality of his voice. The world is different without him. His absence bears a presence all its own. He leaves an emptiness within me that carries great weight.

This is what I now fear most, not being alone but being without an important part of myself. I avoid the eyes of those that I love, wanting to spare them the shocking reflection of emptiness, worried that they somehow will be sucked into the black hole of my despair.

On my own, I search for meaning as if it existed externally. Tahkamenon would laugh at this notion just as he did when I accused him of bringing gems to place along my path. But he is not here, so, full of pride and anger, I reject his thoughts. Maybe he was wrong, or worse, deceitful. Maybe he was distracting me from the true jewels, the ones I could peddle to others, lining my pockets with their wealth.

Consumed with loneliness, I reject his ideas even as I long for his return. I know not why he has left me. I try to remind myself again and again of the times that I thought him gone forever, and then he returned and found me ready to go to new depths, to search the passageways with enthusiasm, not dragging my feet as we reached closer to the core. Yet even as I think these encouraging thoughts, I am not convinced.

Each night I close my eyes against the darkness and search my consciousness for his light. Why has he abandoned me? When will he return? How can I continue if he does not? I try desperately to find the passageways we tread together, illuminated with expectation and discovery. But walls have been erected that block the light and deny me passage. I kick at the bricks and pound upon the cold, dry clay until sweat beads on my forehead and blood trickles down my swollen hands. Despair is no longer abstract, but tangible, squeezing against my organs and threatening my breath.

Sleep is not so much restful as relief. It does not energize, but its necessity allows me brief respite from the emptiness that plagues my waking moments. I feel as if I know not who I am. And although I feel humorless, others still find entertainment in my words. Some do perceive a difference—the weight of my soul noticeable in my actions. But the full impact of the change is mine alone to experience, my burden alone to bear.

Although my loved ones cannot fill the void with their caring, they can warm it briefly with their compassion.

For that, I am eternally grateful.

I finished and stared at the page. Just one week ago, I had no conscious recognition of a relationship with Ta-hkamenon, and here I was writing about the pain of his absence. "How can this be?" I thought, wondering if I was writing about Russ or myself. Neither made sense. If it was me, how and when did I miss someone so desperately that I did not even know that I knew? And if it was Russ, and the reference to finding "entertainment in the words" made me think that it was, why was I writing about his experience in the first person, as if I knew of his emotions, as if I had experienced his pain?

Even worse, here on these pages was none of the ex-hilaration of the first passage. Only darkness and loneli-ness. I was struck by an incredible sadness. I had no immediate desire to share this with Russ or with anyone. I now knew that I could write more, but I did not want to probe the emptiness of these words. Instead, I tried to put the whole issue aside.

The fight with the government was easy refuge from these unsettling thoughts. New challenges sprang to life each day. I spent most of my time on the phone with attorneys, discussing legal strategy and trying not to dwell on the unlimited budget and resources of our regulatory enemies.

I was passionate about the fight. Two years before, gov-ernmental officials had met with me and said that they would welcome litigation to clear up the legal confusion that surrounded the area in which I worked. After months of trying to resolve the issue at hand with meetings and letters and congressional inquiries, our company took the bait. We actually sued the United States Government.

Very quickly we learned our first lesson in Washington logic—just because the officials *said* that they would wel-come a lawsuit, did not *mean* that they would welcome one. Quite the opposite. What we had considered as the next step in our strategy to provide health-care coverage to the uninsured was perceived by the federal government as a declaration of war.

Despite these regulatory problems, our health plan grew rapidly, expanding into new states. This should have been a blessing, but it created a nightmare. Several of the state governments jumped into the fray, forcing us to fight the regulatory battle on a multitude of fronts. While I focused on the federal litigation, the states individually undertook a campaign of daily intimidation and harassment.

I never knew what was going to happen next. One day New York officials would tell participants that we were affiliated with a failed health plan, that we were the target of a very large lawsuit, that we were in fact a scam. The next day New Jersey officials would contact our agents and threaten them with fines or lawsuits. They would tell people that we did not pay our claims or that we only paid the small ones.

I was stunned by all that was happening. The state officials were lying daily, both manipulating the truth and engaging in outright fabrication. We were paying our claims. We were not affiliated with any plan that had previously failed. We were most definitely not a scam. But the truth did not seem to matter. So I dealt with deception day after day.

As the propaganda hit the streets, the phone calls poured in. Our lines flooded each morning with a new round of accusations and innuendo. The participants were scared that they had no coverage. The agents were worried that state representatives were going to break down their doors. The intimidation was intense. Everyone was frightened. Everyone was looking to me for answers. Emotionally it all began to take its toll.

At times I felt like closing the doors and never looking back. I did not own the company, but I did run it. By this time, I was officially the president. I was the one who handled the regulators, who took their phone calls, who responded to their letters, who met them face-to-face when necessary.

While the regulators were rarely personally antagonistic toward me, they were collectively ruthless. When it came to the business at hand, to the fight over territory, there was no retreat. The trench warfare remained intense.

By the time Russ returned from his trip, I was again completely immersed in the fight. Thank heaven he was home. He brought me back to Tahkamenon with his first telephone call. "I'm ready to send some writing," he said. "But I want you to promise to stand by the fax."

I smiled as I recognized the insecurity in his words. "Promise?" I asked. "Don't you trust me?"

"Look, just promise."

"Okay, okay," I responded. "Cross my heart and hope to die."

"Spare me the drama. Just go get the pages."

"All right. I'm going." I reached over to hang up the phone and heard Russ yelling on the other end. I picked it back up to my ear. "What do you want? I'm trying to get to your papers."

"I know. Go. Just call me back as soon as you have them."

"I will. I promise," I said, touched by this rare display of vulnerability. I went out to retrieve his writing, checking in with my staff as I walked through the office. The fax machine rang and then whirred as it spat out page after page. There were twelve in all. I scanned them briefly as I carried them back to my desk.

Maine. Old souls. Puzzles. Truth. Connection. Love.

"This is even more confusing than what I wrote," I thought, folding the papers and calling Russ.

"Did you get them?"

"Yes."

"All of them?"

"Twelve pages."

"Twelve. Only twelve? Just a minute." There was a pause, and I heard Russ shifting through papers. "Yeah that's right. Twelve. Okay. Good."

"I'll read them tonight."

"Whenever," he replied. "I just wanted you to have them."

"Well it's about time."

"Don't even start."

I smiled and changed the subject. "Did you have a good trip?"

"Sure. Fine," he answered. "Just biz. Anything exciting for you?"

"Oh, you know, one or two new lawsuits, a death threat from an insurance commissioner, a strange looking package marked 'destroy if not delivered within five days.' I thought it best not to open it."

Russ laughed. "Good choice. Sounds like nothing's changed."

"Yeah unfortunately," I answered. "I did write some more, though," I added in spite of myself.

"Really? Did you fax it?" I could once again hear him rifling through papers on his desk. "I haven't seen it. Let me just—"

"It's not there. Stop looking," I said, wondering why I had even brought it up. "I'd rather just give it to you when you're down here next week."

"Oh." Russ was silent for a moment. I thought of trying to explain but did not know what to say. "Okay," he said finally. "Suit yourself. Look I've got to go. I just wanted to check in. My desk is swamped."

"Sounds like it," I replied. "Hey, thanks for the writing. I'll call you tomorrow." I was tempted to read his pages, but I had way too much to do. So I tucked them safely away for later.

I had no choice but to turn my full attention back to business. Not only were we losing the battles, we were beginning to lose the war. We were searching for alternatives, but nothing seemed right. The people covered by our plan had little money for insurance. Before our plan, many of the individuals were the uninsured that the politicians had been talking about for three years while doing virtually nothing to deal with the issue of affordability that lay at the heart of the problem. We wanted to find a way to work within the state system and still offer affordable coverage. Everyone we talked with had an answer. Unfortunately, we could not make any of them work.

While searching for a solution, we decided to buy an insurance company. We would find a state with flexible laws and tailor our plan to meet the needs of this group of individuals we had chosen to serve. I put out feelers all over the industry for an available company. Of course I had also turned to Russ. When it came to insurance, he always knew someone who knew someone. He quickly came up with a tempting prospect. Next week he was coming to Virginia to help me review the information and decide if this company could potentially work.

He arrived on Tuesday, and we embraced for the first time since recognizing our connection. The physical closeness was electric. We managed to stay focused on work for the balance of the afternoon but could not wait to put the insanity behind us and talk about our writing and the significance of this new discovery.

Brian watched the kids that evening to give Russ and me time to discuss what was happening. After a quick dinner, we went to Barnes and Noble for coffee and conversation. I gave Russ my latest writing and sat across the small table, sipping cappuccino, trying not to stare. It took him forever to read the passage. I swear I recited it over in my mind four times before he finally put down the papers and looked up.

"You don't like it," I said, disappointed.

"Of course I don't," he responded. "It hurts."

"So, it seems real?"

Russ did not answer but shut his eyes and slowly nodded his head. That was enough. I saw no reason to force the pain of the passage any further into this conversation. Besides, I wanted to talk about what he had written.

I pulled the twelve folded pages from my purse. The words were mysterious—assorted paragraphs and passages written over the past decade, describing important connections. Some of the writing dealt with another old soul that would help Russ solve an important puzzle. The writing spoke of a greater purpose, of finding truth and learning to recognize love. And through it all, it spoke a great deal of Russ's connection with Maine.

"Tell me more about this," I said, holding the papers firmly in my hand.

"What do you want to know?"

"I don't know. Whatever matters." I paused but he did not respond. "Maine seems important," I added.

"Very important," he responded. "Sometimes I think that Maine holds my soul." Russ then spent an hour telling me about Maine, Boothbay Harbor in particular, the character of the people in general. He told the story in his unique way, lapsing into voices, playing out scene after scene in an imaginary general store. He spoke with an affected New England accent that I had to struggle to understand. He spoke with words that were funny and confusing. "She's a good woman, but she makes her beans too hot."

"What are you talking about?" I asked, laughing at the silliness of the statement and noticing that several of the patrons of the small café area were also watching Russ's performance.

"She makes her beans too hot. You know," Russ said, teasing me.

"No. I don't know."

"Well, if you're not from New England, you would just say 'she's a bitch.'"

"That makes absolutely no sense," I responded, laughing and holding up the twelve pages in my hand. "But maybe that explains why this writing is so cryptic."

"Cryptic? Do you think so?" Russ took the pages and glanced over the words. "Funny they make perfect sense to me."

I laid my head on the table in mock exasperation. "I can see that this is going to be a tortuous relationship."

Russ laughed. "Okay, well maybe they are a little puzzling. Puzzling?" he repeated lifting his voice. "Puzzling? Do you get it?"

"Yes I get it," I said, raising my head and shaking it at his reference to the description of puzzles in his writing. "Oh God, now I'm going to have to endure Tahkamenon humor."

"The Big T is incredibly humorous," Russ offered. "He makes me laugh almost every time we speak."

A picture flashed in my mind of this grown man, lying in bed at night, his eyes closed, laughing into the silence. "He really is crazy," I thought, turning back to his writing before fully considering what that implied of my own connection.

The next morning was back to business, so Russ and I put T aside to review financial statements, make phone calls, and set up an appointment to travel to Oklahoma on the following Tuesday to buy an insurance company, we hoped.

"Wow, we're going to see each other twice in two weeks," I remarked, as we prepared to call the travel agent.

"Do you think you can handle it?" Russ asked, swaggering in his chair.

"Let's see," I replied thoughtfully. "I handle the commissioners. I handle the legislators. God knows I have to handle the lawyers." I looked across the desk and smiled. "I think I can find it within myself to handle you."

"They pale by comparison," Russ responded, sliding down into his seat.

We called to arrange the flights. Russ would fly from Philadelphia, I from Virginia Beach. We would meet in St. Louis and fly together to Oklahoma City. I hung up the phone, and we leaned back in our chairs.

"Tahk-a-men-on here we come," I sang quietly.

"Oh listen to you," Russ teased. "Aren't you the one who doesn't believe in this stuff?"

"Of course I don't believe in it," I replied. "I just play along to humor you." We both laughed and turned back to business, each looking forward to next Tuesday with great anticipation.

Chapter Four

I decided to write during the flight. Once in the air, the words poured out onto the paper, spilling over into the margins, flowing from one sheet to the next. Bizarre words and unknown thoughts about adding dimension to linear concepts, the elusiveness of meaning and the quivering tension of zero. I wrote without question, allowing my thoughts to race from one point to the next, not stopping to analyze a sentence or to fill in any of the blanks.

In all that is developed, in each new creation, it is the essence of the third element that sparks the innovation. All that is linear can be but added together or taken away. Only the third plane adds depth and perception. Only from its distance can you distinguish meaning. Only from its existence have you come to know synergy. It is within that energy that you will experience the spirit.

Father, Son, and Holy Ghost—the outward conceptualization of God. It is the attraction to the concept, the magnetic pull of the trilogy, that creates the cohesiveness and basis for much of your formalized religion today.

You have learned to think in threes—a beginning, a middle, an end. You anticipate a third event after two have occurred. You are mystified by the concept of the triangle. Life imitates geometry. You focus on the angles, on the length of the lines. You look to the points for direction but miss the value of the meaning at the center. The rest is repetitive, varying versions of linear relationships converging at preestablished points.

It is the center that is brought into existence by the intersection of the lines. Lines with little meaning, lines easily defined and measured. Segments are created by the triangle, distinguishable by a definable beginning and end. Yet the meaning has little to do with the measurement. The distinction is valuable only as it facilitates comprehension.

What happens to the center when the walls are dismantled? Does it disintegrate? Does it dissipate? Does it leave a discernible trace of what once existed? Elusiveness rests at the center.

The third exists in the meeting of positive and negative, the defining characteristic of zero that is neither plus nor minus but an entity infused with meaning from both sides. Yet the meaning of zero is discernible only from a distance. You perceive its existence more than recognize it. It adds depth to the linear concept, melding all that comes before and all that comes after into a single powerful entity. The parts negate one another, annihilated by a symmetrical opposing force. Only zero is indestructible, strengthened by the pull, quivering with the tension of opposing fields.

Patterns exist within zero, the summation of varying parts. Patterns that provide the key to replacing the tenants of plus and minus, the key to comprehension. It is through the center that you find the light. It is in its midst that you experience understanding.

"Experience understanding?" I thought, as I stopped writing and quickly read the words. "I don't understand any of this stuff." Yet there was an undeniable hint of recognition. I remembered a book that I had been required to read in one of my accounting honors classes at Penn State. It was about finding the pattern that fit. I thought our professor had lost his mind when he assigned it. It was hard to read and had no apparent application to becoming an accountant. But I had thought of it often over the years. There were indeed patterns that fit.

The basic premise of the book was that you should not learn facts discretely. Not only was this basically impossible, but discrete facts held little meaning. You should learn instead to discern the relationship, the pattern that fit the situation. Then when you needed the information again, you could apply it cohesively, needing to remember only the pattern, not each of the individual and varying parts. As I remembered it, the book promised that this would be an exponential increase in our ability to learn and synthesize information. It would make order out of chaos. It had the potential to change our world.

The concept of that book seemed to resonate in these words, which spoke of patterns and numbers. I had always been drawn to figures, especially their relationships. I sensed patterns and trends without consciously recognizing their existence. I thought of Tahkamenon and how hard I was trying to make sense of the individual pieces of the puzzle. "Maybe we should look for the pattern," I thought. "Maybe then we'll find something that fits."

I exited the plane and hurried to Russ's gate. I could not wait to share what I had written and rushed to him with the papers held tightly in my outstretched hand. "You're never going to believe this," we shouted in unison, each holding our writing out to the other. Laughing at the coincidence, we exchanged papers and embraced.

"Let's go get some coffee," Russ said. "We can sit down and look these over. We have about an hour before our next flight."

We found a small coffee shop, ordered, and sat at the front table to read. I unfolded Russ's papers. He unfolded mine. We fell into silence. I focused on his words.

Part of the puzzle of puzzles is your misunderstanding of the concept of three. Your present day understanding is focused on two. Your belief that there are direct opposites has limited your understanding. This concept is linear and constraining.

If plus ten is the opposite of negative ten, then what is zero? If hate is the opposite of love, then what is indifference? Are you beginning to see the limit of the linear plane?

I paused for a moment, amazed by the similarity of our words. I looked up and saw that Russ was absorbed in my writing, so I decided to go on with his:

To understand the force that is the universe, you must understand that there are no opposites, only equal sides of a triangle.

"Holy shit," Russ whispered, breaking my concentration. He stared at me in disbelief. "This is the same stuff."

"I know. I know," I answered, whispering as well. I

waved my free hand in the space between us. "Keep reading," I said. "Just keep reading."

Russ focused on my writing. I turned once again to his.

This is a piece of your first puzzle. Your mind must expand to eliminate the thought process, the belief that everything has an opposite.

You must question that which you think of as known. All of everything must have three sides, three properties, which in total create the basics of its wholeness. Understand that that which you now think of as opposite is truly part of a triangle.

The third dimension breaks the stranglehold of linear thought. There are, of course, more dimensions, but for now, we must speak of the third. It is the third element that provides depth and creates the center. It is that center which allows for the absorption of meaning.

I finished Russ's passage and then read it again while he continued to read what I had written. The third dimension. Opposites. Triangles. Depth. Meaning. The words jumped out at me as I shook my head and stared at the paper.

Russ finished reading and held my writing in his hand. "You just wrote this?" he asked, staring intently and waving the papers slightly in front of me.

"Just now," I answered. "Just like you. I wrote them on the plane." I looked at his writing again and sat back in my seat. "This is weird."

"Yeah, well—more than weird," Russ replied. We were quiet for a moment, each looking again at the other's writing. "Okay," Russ said, rubbing his forehead. "Now I *am* older than you, so just in case I've forgotten—" Russ's voice trailed off as he studied the words.

"Forgotten what?" I said much louder than I had intended, drawing the attention of several people in the cramped coffee shop. "What did you forget?" I quietly asked.

"We've like—" Russ paused and looked away briefly. He turned back and stared into my eyes. "We've never discussed this, have we?"

My voice rose with agitation. "Discussed it Russ? Discussed it? Hell, I've never even thought it." I paused long enough to take a deep breath. "I don't know about you, but it's not like I go around talking about quivering zeros and breaking through linear thought."

"Calm down," Russ said, rubbing the top of my hand.

"You calm down," I replied, pulling away from his touch. "Look at what you've done to me." I shook his papers in front of his face.

"Oh no," Russ responded, laughing and breaking the tension that was growing between us. "You're not going to lay this on me. If you're having a problem here," he added, pointing up into the air as he spoke, "you're going to have to take it up with the big guy."

"Fine," I replied, smiling. "Get him on the line."

"You want me to get him on the line?" Russ asked in amazement. "Hello? Valerie? Have you read this stuff? Don't you think you're already talking to Tahkamenon?"

"No," I answered emphatically. "I am not talking to Tahkamenon."

"Oh yeah," Russ said, rolling his eyes. "I forgot. You don't talk to spirits."

"You're right, I don't. Anyway, for your information, I wasn't talking. I was writing." Russ just looked at me and shook his head. "Now tell him to go away," I added. "I don't want to play anymore."

Russ laid down the papers, picked up his cappuccino and settled back into his seat. "You tell him," he responded.

"He scares me."

We both laughed and then sat again in silence, sipping our drinks and staring off into the space between us. "So everything's a triangle?" I finally said.

"So he says," Russ replied, still looking into the distance. "At least we are."

"We are what?" I asked, irritated by his complacency.

Russ looked at me directly. "Get with the program here, Valerie. You, me, Tahkamenon—a triangle. Don't you get it?"

"No. I don't get any of this. And stop acting so smug. You don't get it either." I maneuvered my chair around our luggage to get closer to Russ. We spread the papers out side by side on the table so that we both could read the words. We sat for a few moments in silence, each glancing from one sheet to the next.

"You're right," Russ said. "I don't get it. This is unbelievable."

"How could we have done this?" I asked. "Why this? And at the same time?" Russ just shook his head, and we both continued reading. "Here," I said, placing my fingers on the two of the papers. "Look at this. 'Only the third plane adds depth and perception.'"

Russ followed the direction of my other hand and read, "the third dimension breaks the stranglehold of linear thought." He leaned closer in toward the table, staring at the writing intently. "Unbelievable," he whispered again.

Chills ran up and down my body, and I shrugged my shoulders to fend off the eerie sensation as they tickled my spine. "Look, look here," I exclaimed, again pointing to sentences from each of our papers.

This time it was Russ who read from my writing. "It is through the center that you find the light."

And I continued from his. "It is that center which allows for the absorption of meaning." I sat back in my seat, noticing that Russ's forearms were covered with goose bumps as well. "I wish he would shed a little more light on what the hell this means," I said.

Russ stayed hunched over the papers. "Life imitates geometry," he read aloud. "I don't know why, but I think that's my favorite part. I guess I should have paid a little more attention in class."

"Don't worry," I responded. "I did. And believe me, we never talked about this. As I remember it, triangles were triangles. No quivering, no meaning, just triangles."

We sat again, without speaking, Russ staring at the writing, I at the moving crowd of travelers as they passed the front of the shop. "This is impossible," I thought, searching for a logical explanation for this incredible coincidence. But even as I tried to consider it a coincidence, my heart resisted. This was no coincidence. It was proof—undeniable proof. If I had doubted our connection at all, to each other, to a greater spiritual force, these similar words and foreign concepts left me with no where to turn but acceptance. If the words had been anything else, anything that we had ever discussed, anything that I had ever thought, then the doubt could have lingered. But not now. Not with this.

I could not look at these words and doubt the connection. Still, I had no idea what that connection meant.

"Oh my God. Look at the time," I said, standing and holding my watch up to Russ's face. "We're going to miss our flight."

"No we won't. Just hurry." Russ stood as well, and we gathered the papers and our luggage and rushed toward the gate. "It's loading," Russ said as we passed the departure monitor. A long line of passengers formed in the distance.

"Where do you think this is going?" I asked as we arrived at the gate.

"Hopefully, Oklahoma City," Russ answered.

"Thanks for the insight," I responded sarcastically. "But that wasn't what I was asking."

"I know," Russ said as we walked down the ramp to the plane. "But that's the only question that I know how to answer."

Once on board, we said little about the writing. We didn't know what else to say. So we focused on business, reviewing the numbers and regulations, analyzing the pros and the cons. In the end, we didn't buy the insurance company. Had it not been for Tahkamenon, that trip to Oklahoma City would have been just one more dead end.

As it turned out, the trip was very much a beginning. It was a flight into our future, a movement into our souls.

Chapter Five

As we accepted the connection, Russ and I were like children on Christmas morning, trembling with anticipation, hurrying to unwrap each brightly colored package. We wrote fragments and sentences, paragraphs and pages, not worrying about their relationship or significance. We rushed to call each other, to share each new insight, to fax each new passage.

Sometimes the writing had direction, sometimes not. We often sensed the meaning without fully understanding the words, so we played with the concepts, allowing them to form more concretely in our minds. We confused our writing with each others, having to resort to the originals to document ownership.

Of course we were not fighting for possession. We were enjoying the connection, this recognition of the attraction each felt toward the other. Now it was even more than that. There were these beautiful words and intriguing ideas that seemed to flourish and flow when we connected our hearts.

Bathe in my beauty, in my radiance. Draw to the center. Warm yourself by the fires of my soul. Refresh in the sparkling streams. My beauty is yours, our radiance of one true source. My rivers flow through you. There are no barriers to the spirit, no meaningful distinctions. Flow freely through my body, through the body of millions, through the universe and into the light.

We read the words and relaxed into their rhythm and bathed in the significance of our connection. It was an incredible awakening, a wonderful gift.

Breathe in the mountains. Bask in their presence. Feel the vibrations, the unity, the connection. From their highest points flows the water that comes to rest at the depths of the ocean. Stand in the midst of the deepest forest, dwarfed by the magnificence, and feel the energy of your presence transform the moment.

But one of many. But of great importance. The paradox of meaning—it is your uniqueness; it is your sameness. Accept them both and find your place within the spirit.

Sometimes we tried to identify ourselves in the words, separate from each other, separate from Tahkamenon. The separation rarely worked. It all made so much more sense when we accepted the writing as a universal application of a universal thought. We grasped the meaning more clearly when we allowed our souls alone to test the significance and held our intellect at bay.

Come to me. I will absorb you into my being. Together we will be whole. We will transcend the barriers, free our souls. As we embrace the moment, we embrace eternity. Join our vibrations. Listen to the song. Pay no attention to the instrument. Focus only on the melody. Experience the creation of light.

Accept the truth that lies within you. It is the same as that which lies within me. Do you not recognize yourself? Look closer. We are not separate. It is an illusion of the physical world. The unity of the spirit enfolds us.

Remove the barriers. Release the fear. Fall into the perfection of your soul.

There were moments of great joy. Russ would call, his voice brimming with enthusiasm. "Hey Val. I talked with Tahkamenon last night. It was wonderful. I tried to put it down. I'm sending you a fax."

And with great anticipation, I would read what he had sent.

Step out. Step out into the light. Become glorious and feel the acceptance of a greater love. Do not let fear overtake you. Stay with the concept that in you, in the universe, the one that loves you most and wishes to love you without fear is there for you now.

The gift I bring lies waiting in your soul. It is a gift that is yours to open. It has your name embossed upon it. Gently remove the ribbon, the wrapping of many colors, and experience the dialogue of the universe. It is the start of your journey. No future day will be as loveless as the past.

This I promise as my gift to you.

"No future day will be as loveless as the past," I thought as I read the passage. "What a truly beautiful gift." Overcome with emotion, I responded:

The truth lies openly, basking in the sunlight. It is your own path that hides it from your view. It is your fear. It is the walls you build first for protection and then for greed that blockade the passage. Remove the walls. Experience the flow.

You build and then pass the blockades on to your children. You must stop the legacy of walls. You have taken the truth and immersed it in fear. It is not altered. It is not forgotten. It is merely covered with your doubt.

Trust is important if you are ever to break through, trust and courage. It cannot happen without eclipsing the barriers of your fear. Truth itself knows no deception. It finds no pleasure in cover.

As always, perfection remains within you, unaltered by your dalliances in the physical world. It is not upon you to create perfection. It is your destiny to accept it.

Because of our work relationship, Russ and I talked daily, mostly about business—operational concerns, the latest obstacles, the newest frustrations. But frequently we returned to Tahkamenon, to the beauty of the message, to the mystery of its source.

I bring no message except for that which exists within you, for we flow from the same spring. It is a basis, an acceptance so simple yet so complex—that you and I are one, each integral parts of the whole.

Russ made a special effort to come to Virginia more often. We would meet during the day for business and steal away moments at night for our writing. Sometimes we would talk about what we had already written, providing little insights, considering the implications of the words. Other times we would sit together and write, feeding off of one another, exploring new depths.

The physical proximity proved magical. We reveled in this new consciousness, exploring the beauty of light and vibrations unrestricted by the boundaries of our rational thoughts. We allowed our minds to push at the edges. We played with the connection. We encouraged our hearts to rejoice.

Often I would pick up on Russ's thoughts or words and unconsciously integrate them into my own. We shared in the surprise as we read over the writing, seeing the likeness, experiencing the connection. Sometimes a word or a phrase would ignite whole passages, page after page streaming from one isolated thought.

Russ wrote:

Like the sun bathes you in light, so too do the stars. They are not a reflection but stand as beacons of communication between your plane and many others.

I read Russ's words and wrote quickly in response:

Star light—the light of darkness. Cool in its radiance, gentle in its touch. It is the light of distant corridors of your being. A light so gentle that it allows you to look directly in. It is the light not of the earth but of the universe. The sun lights your existence in the physical world. The stars light the spiritual.
You need not wish upon their beauty. You need only accept their vibrations. All that you desire, all that you could ask, sparkles from their core, reminding you of the vastness of the universe, allowing for the vastness of your soul.

In the dark stillness of the night, reach out and touch the brightness. Pull it in. Bask in its energy. Be refreshed by the coolness of its caress. There is no reflection. There is no distortion.

What is the truth? What is the message? That the cosmos lies within you. That your spirit knows no boundaries. That you vibrate with both the warmth of the sun and the coolness of the darkness. Neither the night nor the day can withhold your radiance.

The stars are your beacons, reminders that you are never alone. Placed on this planet to be warmed by the sun and cooled by the stars, through your movement not theirs. Your revolution is destined. You have come to learn the limits of your fear. Fear that is of your world only, not of the cosmos. Your fear alone restricts you from your flight and your vibration. With acceptance, with faith, you each will light the path to eternity.

The sun vibrates as one. The stars vibrate as many. You vibrate as both.

The radiance of your smile, the sparkle of your eyes, the soothing of your touch. You are the starlight. You light the darkness with your gentle vibrations. Accept your place within the cosmos, within the spirit. Allow the significance to flood your being.

As always the answer is simple—the power of the stars lies within you, the power of the spirit innate.

"Simple?" we challenged as we read these passages and discussed the words. "Simple? The answer may be simple to you, Tahkamenon, but please be patient. We're struggling a little here just to hang on." And struggle we did, with the elusiveness of the words, with the pain of our human existence, with the intensity of our joint desire to give voice to the vibrations of our souls.

It was beautiful, yes. Inspiring, awesome. But simple? Never. As we faithfully worked to reconcile these words with our humanity, we found the message anything but simple.

Chapter Six

"Hello. This is Valerie," I said quickly, angry that the phone rang just as I was leaving for home.

"Hey Val, it's Russell. You're never going to believe this."

I sat on the back of my desk and leaned over it, the light already off in my office, my purse in my hand. "Try me. But make it fast. I have to get Ashleigh to soccer practice."

"God. Is it Thursday already? I can't believe—"

"Russ! Tell me what you want. I have to go."

"Okay, but this is important. Do you remember my dream?"

"Could you be more specific?"

"You know. I've told you before. I've had this one dream all my life about walking to the water as a child with a little girl holding my hand."

"Yeah. I remember," I said, straining my neck to see the clock. My heart sagged with guilt. "Ashleigh is going to kill me," I added.

Russ continued excitedly, ignoring my comment. "There is always this incredible moment when the light reflects off of the water, and they can't see anything but its radiance."

"Russ, does this have a point? I really have to go."

"I can never see the girl. She's always there. Every time. But we're walking side by side so I never see her face."

I quietly pulled the keys from my purse, praying for light traffic.

"Val. Are you there? Are you listening?"

"Yes. Russ, I've got to go. I'll call—"

"No. Wait." His voice trembled with emotion. "I saw her. I finally saw her face."

"Great. That's really great. I've got to go. I'll call you tonight. I promise." I leaned over further to hang up the phone.

"It's you," Russ whispered. "It's always been you."

I sat back up and pulled the phone closer to my ear. "Are you sure?" I asked as my eyes welled with tears.

"I'm positive."

"Wow." His statement stunned me. But Ashleigh was waiting. I didn't know what to do. "Russ look, I . . . I'm really sorry. I have to get Ashleigh. I'll call you tonight."

"We're going out tonight, but that's okay. I've been in a meeting all day, and I just had to tell you. Call me tomorrow."

"Okay. Tomorrow then," I replied, suddenly reluctant to hang up the phone. "Russ."

"Yes?"

"I'm glad that I'm in your dream," I said, wiping a tear from my cheek. I had to say something. It wasn't much, but it was the best I could do.

"Me too," Russ responded softly. "Now go get Ashleigh. She'd never forgive me if I made her late for practice."

"She'd never forgive either of us," I responded. "I'm going."

"Val," Russ added quickly. "I love you."

"Yeah, me too," I answered before hanging up and running out to my van.

"First the airport and now this," I thought, as I drove to pick up my daughter and replayed the conversation with Russ in my head. I did remember him telling me about the dream before. It was one of the few times he had spoken of Vietnam, about how hard it was at night with the rain and the bugs and the uneasy silence that could be broken at any moment by bullets.

It was in this context that he had spoken of the dream's comfort, of its beauty, of its light. He had said there was a girl with him, two children walking together toward the water. At the time, I did not question who she was. She was just a girl, and it was just a dream. But now the girl was me, and the dream seemed more—more proof of our connection, more beauty for our souls.

Over the next few weeks, we talked a great deal about the dream. Russ described more fully the times when he had had this vision in his life. It comforted him. It intrigued him. He had often wondered who the child was. Was it his wife, his daughter, any of a multitude of friends? Yet nothing had seemed to fit until now. And for all the years of questioning, it took only one glance to be convinced.

As Russ described the beauty of the dream, the connection between us again found expression in my words. I wrote as if I were Russ, and we again sensed a meaning that we could not quite comprehend.

I see her now, not as she stands before me, but as a child, holding my hand in the sunlight.

So many memories, flooding together, each diminishing the borders of the others until the colors settle into a carpet of yellow and purple haze. Hand in hand, we cross the fields, covered to our waists by the flowers, rustling in the rhythm of the breeze. Our own colors, reflected in the radiance of the sun, cast brilliant, multicolored shadows in our wake.

The lake vibrates in our presence; its dimensions springing to life as we approach, shades of blue and green and brown intensifying to reveal hidden depths. We point in unison to the movements in the water, impossible to notice from the distance, camouflaged by the surface, protected from those who never venture close to the water's edge.

We continue forward until the moment of impact, the total blindness of the light reflected from the water, blocking all perception, flooding our senses with its warmth.

Euphoric, we close our eyes and lie back into the lushness of the bank, raising our faces to the comforting warmth. We listen intently to the echo of the ripples, the swoosh of the fish, the distinct vibrations of the crickets, separate in their tenor yet in harmony with the symphony of the lake. Lying side by side, our torsos touching, we soak in the smell of damp grass, and wildflowers, and sunlight, allowing the aroma to permeate our being.

Suspended by the pleasures of the physical world, we hold our motion, neither wanting to displace the movements of this moment, both unsure of the impact of the ripples. The intensity of the mixture of the water and the light flows through our bodies, calming our hearts and energizing our souls.

In time the child at my side opens her mouth and sings with words and a voice not of her being alone but of us both and of the coolness of the lake and the warmth of the breeze and the movement of the fish and the fragrance of the flowers.

Tears warm my cheeks, salty as they fall in rivulets down my face. The melody overtakes my being, forcing my heart to beat fast against my chest, freeing my soul to soar past the tops of the tall, thin pines bordering the distance.

Time continues without our knowledge, as if the day were but a single, perfect moment in our lives.

Eventually, the sun drops on the horizon, cooling the breeze and spreading dramatic streaks of pink and orange to decorate the sky. The water calms, its silence broken only by the occasional gulp of a fish surprising a stray minnow skimming near the glassy surface. And then the ripples start again, setting off new movements, uncontemplated by the fish in his sole pursuit.

My body damp with the perspiration of the grass, my face taut with the salty remains of dried tears, I hold the child peacefully at my side, the song no longer flowing from her lips. We rise to leave in twilight, illuminated with the essences of the moment and of the song and of the light, each revealed in its own distinct way.

And in my wakening, I see her now, a woman, not realizing that I feel the impression of the tiny hand in her touch and hear the echo of a sacred song within her voice.

I have come to this picture often, first as a child and now as a man. Each time I find exhilaration, leaving refreshed and hopeful, desirous of capturing the words of the song.

Together we will find a way to release the message. The song is louder now. I perceive, if not quite understand, the wisdom in the mysterious words, flowing at the inspiration of the physical world from a place deep within our being.

Soon she too will hear its rhythm and will be swept away by the melody. I trust that she will remember the vibration, that the connection of many lifetimes will once again be understood.

During the weeks that followed, we each wrote more about the dream, trying to analyze its meaning, trying to absorb its significance.

It is a message of connection. To each other. To yourself. To the physical world. To your spiritual being. A message of harmony of the senses. The melody of the voice—emanating from a single source, infused with meaning from each element of being, vibrating with life.

Hold the hands of the children. Feel the warmth of their souls reflecting back on the sun, increasing its radiance. The smell of the wildflowers intensified by the mustiness of the grass, by the stirring of the breeze. The connection with the universe intensified by the harmony of the vibrations. The elements brought into alignment, each recognizing the placement of the others, rejoicing in the synergy of the arrangement. It is a melody that breaks the barriers of language, eclipsing the distinctions between plant and animal, equalizing the existence of the lake and the fish and the flowers and the children. A total communion of being. Each one experiencing the others fully, joyous in the knowledge that their joint existence brings.

The power of the moment is the harmony of being. The integration of the light and the water and the creatures and the children. It is a moment void of walls. More secure than any other you have ever known, full of the expectations of innocence.

After stopping long enough to read these words, I finished with the following:

What are we to make of this connection? Together we create the voice, the song of wisdom to enlighten those who will open their minds and listen with their hearts.

By the time I was ready to share these ideas with Russ, he had his own to share with me.

Tahkamenon sings a tale of time not recorded but of moments remembered as wildflowers, basic and stray under a cloudless sky. He whispers in my ear a shout of silent peace. I am comforted and encouraged. He comes to me as the sun rising above the horizon awakens the flowers of the garden, transforming dew into light.

And before we were able to put the dreamscape behind us, I wrote still more of the importance of the song:

Music penetrates walls. Maybe those who do not hear the words will begin to move to the rhythm of the music and find comfort in the ancient beat of the drums. The tune will be familiar—a song that you know but cannot remember, a song that you hum without comprehending the words.

Have faith in the melody. Listen to the lyrics, words existing for centuries yet newly created. Transformed by your being, conforming to your level of acceptance yet never altering from their course.

You not only hear the song but also add to it. Accept your place within the harmony. One place, many places, energized and unrestrained. Do not fear the message. Lift your voice in song. Infuse your life with meaning. Immerse your heart in love.

I asked a great number of questions regarding the dream but never voiced the one that intrigued me the most. When did this start, this dream of connection? According to what I had written, "first as a child and then as a man." But that could not be. I was almost twenty years younger than Russ. If he had this dream as a child . . . no. It was impossible. Maybe it was now me. But then? Then I was not even . . . I could not finish the sentence, not even in my head.

So I moved forward and let the question lie, already answered in the depths of my soul. I walked through the dream as if it were my own, smelling the flowers, basking in the warmth of the sun. Mostly I reveled in the connection, treasuring its security and light.

We accepted the dream as a scene that united us, a symbol that embodied our connection, not just to each other, but to the whole of our existence, to our surroundings and, most importantly, to our source.

Chapter Seven

What we welcomed as an incredible gift soon became also an undeniable curse. We fell into a rhythm of parallel lives, both with each other and within ourselves. Each accepted a new allegiance toward the other that extended beyond friendship and that penetrated our souls. We felt an overwhelming responsibility to a message that we did not fully understand, to words and ideas that we worked to form and document and synthesize into our lives.

But how to incorporate writing that defied our definitions, that spoke of foreign feelings, that voiced opinions we were unsure how to embrace?

The pyramids were given as a sign, as a remembrance of existence without barriers. You built them with your understanding but distracted yourselves by using them to encase physical wealth. They were not intended to house the wealth. They are the wealth.

You view the pyramids with wonder, not surprise, for you knew them always to exist. Have you not moved barriers as large within yourself? There are many more to move. Some larger than others. Each difficult in its own way. But all possible—that is the message. You needed not sophistication or technology or education to build the pyramids. Just belief.

What greater gift than the knowledge that the physical world holds no true barriers? That even massive stones flow freely in the faith? In their purest form, the pyramids represent a total lack of fear. They are by definition the very omission of doubt.

Foolishly, with distraction, you filled the pyramids with your fear—precious jewels and gold bullion, false representations of wealth, beauty displayed only in reflection. They do not sparkle in the darkness. They do not vibrate with the intensity of light.

You do. You vibrate with the light of the universe. Do not work so hard to block the flow.

"The pyramids," I said to Russ after sending this passage. "Why am I writing about pyramids? I don't know anything about pyramids."

"Aren't you listening?" Russ asked, his voice confident and condescending. "It seems to me that you know everything about pyramids."

I hated Russ when he was like this, when he pretended that it all made sense. I knew that by tomorrow he would again be questioning, yet I feared that maybe he now got the message, and I alone was searching in the dark.

I was baffled by the poetic words and powerful phrases. Even if we accepted their spiritual significance, how could we apply them here? What were we to do amid the turmoil of our careers, the needs of our families, the fight with the government, the endless struggle within ourselves? What was it that Tahkamenon wanted? What purpose could all of this possibly serve?

We received few answers, but the words continued, and their very existence cried out for action, for a way to be heard. Propelled forward by the beauty and authenticity of the writing, we encountered our fears and questioned our beliefs. As we tuned in to vibrations of our souls, the thoughts flowed from our being, the love poured from our hearts.

Come to me in the darkness, in the stillness of the night. Come without fear, without barriers. Draw in to the vibration and know that you are not alone. That you are never alone. You are one with the spirit. We are one with each other. Release the distinctions. Release the distractions. Meaning does not generate from the physical world. You have tried to infuse it with significance but it has left you empty, cut off from the power of the source.

And in the void stand the shadows of your fear. You have removed yourselves from the universal flow. You have cut yourselves off from the light but have not altered the vibrations of the truth. The light continues. The melody remains. You need only fall within its rhythm.

You see the truth still in glimmers. You hear it in whispers when you are quiet and the barriers allow some room for movement. You know when it touches close to your heart.

Tear down the walls. Do not be afraid of the truth. Do not doubt your ability to understand. You understand already. You need only accept the understanding.

None of this was easy, but there was no holding back in the end. We resisted and then gave in to our own curiosity. We decided to trust, to let the words flow, to allow ourselves to believe. It wasn't absolute. The doubt was inevitable. But it lost both its intensity and duration as we listened to the whispering of our souls.

Everything felt different, exhilarating, whole. We thrived on the connection and missed it deeply when we fell out of sync. What we feared would add extra duties to our already staggering routines added instead extra significance, gave meaning to our existence, and helped us to make it through the relative torment of each day.

Of course Russ and I had to rework our relationship. We were two wholly different physical beings sharing a special spiritual bond. No matter how deep the connection, we still crossed paths with some degree of difficulty here in the physical realm. It was always with a sense of agitation that we got together. We both saw the big picture but agreed little on the individual steps.

We tripped over each other a great deal, each choosing a different way to move us further along the path. We had differing ideas, spoke with varying voices. As we tried to form the writing into something more akin to a book, passion surrounded every issue from the title, to the format, to the order.

At times we seemed to agree on everything and nothing. It was wonderful and impossible, freeing and condemning, all wrapped up into one mind-bending, life-altering event. We had become partners of little choice, more like kin than friends, drawn together by an inexplicable fate.

We did not disagree as to the message. The message was. It existed. Its meaning transcended us. Its beauty enfolded us. But always the question—what to do with these powerful words? Not only did we fail to agree with each other, we often failed to agree within ourselves—changing positions at each turn, viewing each angle as the answer until we quickly moved on to the next.

One day I would support keeping the story just between us, and Russ would want to write a book. The next he would relegate the message to the confines of our friends, and I would be planning Oprah appearances and a multi-city promotional tour. Just as with the incredible turmoil we were facing with business, the haphazard and ever-shifting context drew us together, learning to trust in each other's intentions and believe in each other's heart.

Still, there remained moments of darkness—many moments when the struggle to find our way seemed to overwhelm the beauty of the message. There were even times when I resented the message, teasing me with its serenity while turning my world upside down in its wake. Russ too had doubts. We counted it as a blessing that usually only one of us was doubtful on any given day. Yet even in these moments of doubt, we could not deny the incredible significance of the words.

We were careful to whom we told the story, often leaving out key details in an attempt to make the situation more palatable. I fought what was happening much harder than Russ did. I worried more about what others would think. Still, we both worried a great deal.

We were concerned about our families and how this would affect them. Even our connection was cause for concern. Why was this happening between us? We knew that the connection was long term, but would Brian and Mary Ellen understand this unusual commitment? Would they feel jealous? Would they accept our passion for the message that inevitably spilled over into a relationship that neither of us could fully explain? And what of our children?

Would this message bring them joy or sorrow? Would our responsibility draw us away from them in a way that we would never accept from our jobs?

Most of all we worried about what to do next. Were these words for words' sake, thoughts and understandings meant for our enjoyment alone? We believed that Russ had the most direct connection with Tahkamenon, so we decided that he should ask. He did and then spent night after night waiting for a reply.

Finally Tahkamenon responded.

How should you choose to write your parable? With or without your Tahkamenon? Who does or doesn't exist? It is your choice. It is your parable. How tell you the story?

"Damn it, Tahkamenon. That's what I am asking you?" Russ replied. "What do you want us to say? And who are we supposed to be saying it to?" Russ tried to hold his agitation in check, fearing Tahkamenon would not speak if he sensed the tone of the question. But again came the beautiful voice, the meaningful words.

Think of me as an instrument, a flute, and realize that when we talk, when we make music, I am the instrument and you the musician. So it is for Valerie as well. But realize always that I too play you as an instrument. And so to make music, our vibration is beautiful. Our job—to play for others.

Should I be a guitar, a harp, a piano? So I can, and so can you. This moment you see me only as one instrument and you see yourself as only one as well. Listen. The sound is so beautiful, but it is the sound of but one instrument. The lesson—think of yourself as an orchestra.

Ah, so many instruments. You do not realize you can play them all in harmony, a melodious tune. Expand your thinking to think of yourself as not just one manifestation but many.

Are you not a father, a son, a husband, an uncle, a nephew, a cousin, a friend? Are you not different but the same? Oh Russell, were you to play all of your parts in harmony, what a beautiful song your life would play. Play these parts in disharmony and what discord in your life. If it is harmony you so choose, you must play more than one instrument. Play loved. Play with love.

Can you hear it? Far, far away. Turn up the volume. Learn to do this. Practice until the song of love can make the singing bird listen to your chirping and the flowers bend with your rhythm.

Remember this. This is a parable about light and vibration. Think of it as such and glean from it the lesson.

For today I am the father and you the son. Tomorrow it shall be different, but for now we have today.

There was a pause and Russ expressed his gratitude. It was not an answer really, but it was something. "To play for others," Russ thought, turning the idea over in his mind. Still unsure of the message, Russ now felt a new conviction that these words were not for our ears or our hearts alone. And before the encounter was over, Tahkamenon again whispered to his soul.

I teach you nothing new. I only open your heart to let you hear old melodies. I do this with love.

"And I accept it with love," Russ responded. He quickly rose to write the words as best he could. He called me the next morning, excited yet somewhat confused.

"It all seemed so clear last night," he started as soon as I had the words before me and we were again talking on the phone.

"What beautiful words," I responded. "'Both instrument and symphony.' It makes sense doesn't it?"

"To play for others," Russ said. "I think that answers our question."

"It does seem to say that it's not just for our pleasure alone. But he still doesn't tell us where to go from here."

"He never does."

"Great," I responded. "You could have at least found a spirit who came with instructions."

Russ laughed. "I can never follow those damned instructions anyway." We both sat quietly, reading over the words. Eventually Russ broke the silence. "I guess some things are better figured out for yourself."

Unfortunately, I was not feeling so resolved. I loved what Russ had written, and I was glad that he was happy, but I wanted to know precisely what was expected. I wanted my own answers. I wanted some peace.

During this time of intense questioning, I woke before the alarm one morning and lay in bed thinking of all that had happened. The story never failed to amaze me, to move me, to confuse me—so much insight and still no direction. It angered me to think that I had a new responsibility without any explanation of what it entailed.

I shut my eyes again, against the early morning light, sinking back into the pillow and allowing my thoughts to drift. They rambled through the fragments of my mind and halted on a dramatic visualization. It was an antique writing quill, a yellowed parchment scroll and a small pot of black ink. The quill glided across the paper, slowly and smoothly, with no visible manual guidance. The penmanship was large and scrawling but perfectly legible, incredibly clear:

If you have the courage to write the message, I have the courage to tell it.

"Tahkamenon?" I quietly gasped, sitting straight up in bed and opening my eyes. The picture vanished as the light rushed in. I dropped my head into my hands and rubbed the sockets around my eyes. "Tahkamenon?" I asked silently, half-expecting a reply.

None came. I pulled a notebook from my nightstand and quickly wrote down the words. I had seen them written, as they actually were being formed, flowing before me with all of their beauty and strength. I immediately thought the words were in response to my questioning. "But courage? Courage?" I asked, more confused than before. "What the hell does that mean?"

Unfortunately this was one time that I would not have to wait long for an answer.

Chapter Eight

It was a Sunday morning—at our house that means my husband's famous homemade pancakes. I am convinced that friends and relatives visit just to satisfy their cravings for Brian's delicious creations, a legacy of love from his mamaw's southern kitchen. Much to the delight of our children, he makes them to order in the shape of letters or cartoon figures. Once you've attended this Sunday morning ritual, you're hooked for life.

This morning was different. Oh I ate the pancakes—even a special one decorated with chocolate chips—but I didn't really enjoy them. It wasn't Brian's fault. I'm sure that the pancakes were wonderful, the ceremony as loving and indulgent as always. The pancakes were not the problem. It was me. My mind was racing. My heart felt light and fast. I could not concentrate even long enough to taste. I just shoveled and swallowed, thanked my husband, cleared my plate, and excused myself from the table.

I needed to get upstairs to write and release the restless energy I had barely held at bay during breakfast. Again it was a sentence that permeated my consciousness, an intriguing fragment of what I suspected to be a much longer thought:

> I come to you not as a heretic but as a believer; we both believe in love.

Afraid to focus on the words before I was ready to transcribe them onto paper, I rushed to my room, closed the door, crawled onto my bed and wrote.

> I come to you not as a heretic but as a believer; we both believe in love.
>
> I wonder at the confines of formalized religion—of the oppression of the walls, of the blocking of the light. We are all but one messenger. In truth there is but one voice.
>
> Only fear has blocked the faith. A fear that fosters rules. And walls. Walls that grow upon each other until the movement of the light is fragmented. Until you no longer stand directly in its vibration. Until you no longer bask in its security and warmth. You have come to know your soul only through reflection.
>
> You fail to understand that these rules of your religions are based on fear, imply fear, instill fear. And fear allows no room for faith. It is a gradual process; a little fear blocks a little faith. But it is comprehensive, gaining momentum. With time the blockage becomes thicker and more destructive.
>
> Can you not see the inverse nature of your actions? Men of God should speak of God and not of rules. Jesus was crucified by your fears. Yet those who came after distorted his message and allowed that same fear to create

false beliefs, to place false importance. In the spiritual world, what is the importance of a day of the week, a manufactured altar, or a piece of food that provides nourishment that serves only to sustain the body with no relevance to the soul? You have become distracted. You have distorted even the reflections.

Love thy neighbor is not a rule; it is a message. It is an understanding. It rests easily close to the heart. It is energizing and filled with light. It eclipses the barriers of the physical world. It overshadows the need for the commandments. For if you infuse your life with love, which implies understanding, acceptance, and energy, there is no need for the rules.

Thou shalt not kill. Honor thy father and mother. Thou shalt not commit adultery. These are rules, displays of doubt in the truth. If you trust in the loving, then you have no need for the rest. The rules are more harmful than helpful. They allow the doubt to enter. They release the fear. They impinge upon the faith.

Fear grabbed hold of my lungs as I wrote the words. My heart raced. My mind wandered from the paper until I chased it down again and manually forced it back on track. "How can I say these things about religion?" I silently asked. This was heresy. Or at least it looked like heresy. Still I knew that it was true. We had beaten our faith with rules, leaving nothing but fear, and lingering echoes of our doubt. Immediately I saw the truth. Immediately I feared the repercussions.

Trembling, I read and reread the words. "The Ten Commandments have been more harmful than helpful?" I thought. "Lock the doors. Barricade the house." I feared not the words but the reaction. I wanted to run from the heresy of the page, to disown it, to somehow disbelieve.

"The opinions expressed by this writing are not necessarily those of the writer," I wanted to shout to the world. But they were mine and I did believe—fully, truly, absolutely. Each test that I could derive failed to show a weakness, a break in the logic, a glimmer of deceit.

"What is the need for rules if we truly hold love?" I asked as I tested each commandment. Each time it was the concept of love and not the rule that held true. Love made far more sense than the dogma. In this context, I could view the rules only as expressions of doubt. "Love thy neighbor—but in case that does not work, do not kill, steal, lie, covet, and so on." I tried again and again, but I could not think of the rules and still trust in the love. The rules read like a fine print disclaimer, our signal that love is not really what it proclaims itself to be.

Here on paper, in my hurried, scrawling hand, was just the reverse. It was the belief that love was everything, that these rules of our religions, rules made by man not God, could only diminish the power, could only cover the light.

My thoughts were interrupted by the need to put my pen back to the paper.

Do you not see the barriers your rules have created? Do you not perceive the suffocation of the faith? If we are of one source, then rules that end in exclusion can not bring you closer to the spirit.

"Yes, yes, Tahkamenon," I answered into the silence, unable even with my fear to deny the authenticity of the words. "I do see the barriers. I do feel the suffocation of the faith."

Again I read the words, falling into their rhythm, slipping into my past. I saw myself as a child, sitting in the pews of the ornate Catholic church of my rural Pennsylvania town. It was much more splendid than my own simpler

Methodist church. More stained glass, more statues, more candles, more rules. And, so I thought with the logic of my youth, more God.

Even the priest was more decorated, further removed from the congregation. I was in awe of this church and thought that God must surely be here. I was drawn to the ritual, to the words spoken in unison, to the claims of faith and the cleansing of sin. I came to the Catholic church often, reveling in the pageantry, strangely drawn to the rigidity of the faith.

I wanted to be Catholic. I worked hard to blend in. I bought a set of rosary beads and practiced Hail Marys. I loved those beads, powder blue with a simple silver cross. I believed they could work miracles. I believed they allowed me to speak directly to God.

In my effort to belong, I memorized prayers. I knelt on cue. I knew when to sing and when to shake hands. "Peace be with you. And also with you." But I was not Catholic. I did not go to catechism. So I had to pick up the rules as I went along and ended up with my own interpretation of what God required of the Catholic faith.

The weekly confession and communion intrigued me most. It seemed no matter your actions or missteps throughout the week, no matter your hatreds or meanness, you could enter a magical chamber, draw a black curtain, relinquish your sins and be saved from their impact. Each Sunday morning, I watched the mystical parade as the chosen ones stood row by row and filed toward the alter to cleanse their souls with the body and blood of Christ. Thankfully, grape juice and round wafers were the symbolic substitutes for what I initially thought a dreadful penance.

The priest held the goblet. Anointed assistants helped with the wafers. Everyone spoke in whispers, and the congregation knelt in prayer. The recipients shuffled past as they returned to their seats, allowing the bread to melt in their mouths. No one ever chewed. I decided the magic must need to be released slowly. I watched in awe at the transformation, grape juice and bread able to wash away even the most offensive of sins. What power. What hope. As I was soon to find out, what guilt and what pain.

I watched for months, my curiosity rising. I had taken communion at my own church, but this was not the same. Our communion was sporadic, not weekly. Our salvation was not dispensed from a beautiful golden goblet carefully wiped with white linen by a heavily adorned priest. We drank instead from sip-size plastic cups that were retrieved and returned to small round holes on a circular platter. Yes I had taken communion, but I had never partaken in this intriguing Catholic ceremony.

So one day, unable to fight my curiosity any longer, I rose. Watching those ahead of me carefully, mimicking their actions, I received the drink and the wafer. I returned to the pew and knelt in prayer, thanking God that I did not trip or otherwise disrupt this solemn event. Not much happened. I still felt the same. Maybe since I hadn't done anything really sinful that week, I was not getting the full effect. Still it was nice to belong, to feel the wafer melt on my tongue as I knelt on the red velvet padding of the wooden prayer bar.

After church my new sense of belonging was shattered. A lady from the congregation came up to me on the sidewalk. She was pleasant at first, asking after my mother. Then her eyes narrowed. "When did you take your first communion?" she asked.

My stomach turned. "I haven't," I replied. "I'm not Catholic. I just love to come to this church."

"But I thought I saw you taking communion," she said, her voice rising with the accusation.

"No. You couldn't have," I stammered. "It wasn't me," I added, panicking and wiping away any remaining value the communion could possibly have held for my soul. I turned and walked away quickly, not looking back, denying her a chance to respond.

"Oh my God, you have to be Catholic," I thought, my heart pounding as I hurried home. "How did I miss that rule?" In my church, anyone who wished to repent their sins and welcome Christ into their hearts could partake. Obviously that was not the case here. "How could this be?" I thought. "God only forgives Catholics?" Even at twelve, I found that rule just too impossible to believe.

I returned the following Sunday to my own Methodist church, proud of our inclusion. But I began to recognize our rules of exclusion as well. I began to question. I began to doubt. I came to church hungry, wanting to nourish my soul and fill my heart. I left with the rules, with the guilt, with the terrifying stories of hellfire and damnation.

Still I held on to the ideal. I continued to believe in God and learned to separate the beauty of his being from the isolation of the rules. But I felt like an impostor. Church eventually just dwindled away. I went from time to time, but it unfolded like a play. I went not for the religion but for the momentary solace. The outside world seemed to stop at its doors, worries unable to penetrate the sacred power of stained glass.

I never did return to that beautiful Catholic church. It was too painful. I had been embarrassed and betrayed. I had gone looking for love and forgiveness and was denied both as a matter of principle. According to the lady with contempt in her eyes, I did not qualify for her God.

Now, over twenty years later, I sat in my room with these words in my hands, reliving the impact of the rules of exclusion.

I come to you not as a heretic but a believer; we both believe in love.

I cried as I reread the words, stung by their authenticity. No pageantry. No pretext. A club so open that the whole world would not be enough to hold all those invited. It would take more. It would take the heavens as well.

I ran downstairs to Brian and handed him the words. I no longer worried that he would not love me. I wanted his reaction. I wanted his reassurance that I could go on. He was unloading the dishwasher—our children running in and out of the kitchen in search of shin guards and cleats, a soccer game forming in our backyard. Brian took my papers and went to the kitchen table to read.

After a few minutes, he looked up at me and said nothing.

"Should we lock the doors?" I asked.

"That won't be enough," he replied as he slowly shook his head.

"Do you want me to quit?"

"Never," he answered without hesitation. "Anyway, it doesn't look to me as if you have much of a choice." Brian rubbed his fingers down the pages. "The Ten Commandments, huh? Boy, when you pick a fight, you really pick one." He smiled, rose and walked toward me. "I guess the federal government just isn't enough of a challenge," he said laughing. "Now you have to go after God."

"I'm not," I cried, pushing him back as he tried to hug me. "Stop it. I'm not picking a fight. This isn't against God. This is *for* him. Don't you see?"

"Yeah," Brian said, pulling me close against my resistance. "But I have a feeling there's a lot of people who won't."

"I know," I whispered as I relaxed against his body. "I keep waiting for the lightning bolt."

"Well, get away from me then," Brian exclaimed, releasing his hold.

"Brian," I yelled, losing my balance.

He quickly caught me and pulled me again into his arms. "I'm not going anywhere," he said. "You just keep writing." Brian held me close. "I'm going to hold tight, lightning bolts and all."

Even with Brian's reassurance, the fear rushed in. I was afraid not just for myself but also for my family. Brian could agree to move forward, but what about my children? Angry zealots have little history of discretion. The fear was overwhelming until I caught myself in this self-induced frenzy.

"Stop it," I silently demanded. "Who is going to care what you have to say anyway? Don't be so full of yourself."

The question worked. A little. Logically this made sense. Who was I to question the Ten Commandments? My knowledge of theology was much like my childhood knowledge of Catholicism. I knew what I saw, what felt right, and what didn't. But that was all. I couldn't debate the bible. I couldn't quote scripture or recite many prayers. Who was I?

But these questions were of my mind only. My heart continued onward with little doubt as to my purpose, with little concern for my lack of formal qualification.

Still feeling uneasy, I decided to call Russ. He would calm me down. Autumn answered. Her parents were sleeping. So much had happened that I hadn't even realized that it was only 10:00 a.m., midmorning in our household but still early in theirs. "No, no, that's okay. Don't wake them. I'll call back later." I hung up and asked Brian if he minded if I went out for a walk.

It was an overcast morning, but the sun was beginning to peek through the clouds. Although it hadn't rained, the ground was damp from the dew that was burning off slowly. I walked a long circle around my neighborhood, questioning everything that was happening.

As was becoming my habit, I tried to explain the story to myself.

"Okay," I thought, "so I meet this guy in business. We are both go-getters, very focused. We love our families, try to balance our priorities. Brian's dead father visits me. I tell Russ. He tells me about his conversations with the Big T. I write about the details. We fly into an airport at the same time on different planes and both write about zero quivering and life imitating geometry. We accept that we are connected. We continue to exchange writing. We finish each other's thoughts. We receive a beautiful message." And this morning I could not help but add, "We trash religion, and our worlds come tumbling down."

The story itself was still unbelievable when I reduced it this way in my mind. I imagined everyone I knew and loved turning away as I revealed that we were talking with dead people. "And now we have to beat up on the Ten Commandments," I thought. Even if I could accept the rest of the story, this new ending distressed me. "Why does even the message have to be controversial?"

Walking through the neighborhood, I was struck again by my arrogance. "Who am I, who are we, to proclaim this message?" Before I could even finish forming the question, the answer was drowning out all of my doubts. "The arrogance is in accepting the Ten Commandments, not in questioning them." I continued to walk, step after step, the houses and playground, the cars and the people, all static in the background as I focused solely on my thoughts.

I listened to the words, unsure where they came from, fearful of where they led.

"Haven't you been evolving for millions of years?

Physically, intellectually, socially? Even the rules you now accept as God's have evolved over time. Why should you believe that you now have the answers? Do you not recognize that your spiritual evolution goes hand and hand with the rest?"

Suddenly, one man caught my attention as I walked the final stretch to my house. He stood across the street, his golden retriever held on a leash, the back of his head tilted upward as he stared over a small man-made lake and up toward the sky.

Intrigued by his stillness, I followed his gaze. There, over the lake, was the faintest of rainbows, breaking through the clouds and lightly reflecting on the water below. I stood still as well, and the colors intensified under our gaze, he on one side of the road, I on the other. Cars slowed as they passed between us, passengers craned their necks to look skyward, spontaneously following our lead.

"How could this be?" I asked myself. "A rainbow? But it hasn't rained?" I asked only once. The answer did not seem to matter for it certainly existed—a beautiful rainbow parting the clouds. A gift from the heavens. A message of hope.

I walked home, stunned by the coincidence. I had been searching for a sign, a way of knowing that I was on the right track. And just when I heard an undeniable voice telling me that my questions were not heresy, I found a rainbow without the requisite rain.

My home came within view. I turned and looked once more at the sky behind me. The rainbow remained, even larger and brighter than before. I ran the rest of the way to my husband and children, who were out back, playing soccer. I interrupted the game. They all stopped to appreciate the rainbow. My rainbow. Of course I didn't tell them that I believed it to be mine.

"Cool Mom. When did it rain?" Eric asked.

"It didn't."

"But I thought it had—"

"Eric kick the ball," Ashleigh interrupted. "I'm still winning."

"No you're not. You're cheating," Eric replied. "Mom, Ashleigh's cheating."

"Why don't you both just try to enjoy the game for a change?" I asked, heading back toward the door.

"I am enjoying it," Ashleigh said, smiling broadly. "I'm winning."

Seeing that she was distracted, Eric quickly kicked the ball in the goal. "There," Eric said triumphantly. "Now it's tied."

"Mom," Ashleigh screamed. "That's not fair."

"It's not always fair, honey. Sometimes you just have to take it as it comes." I opened the back door to slip into the house. "Now enjoy the game."

As I shut the door, my own voice rang through my head, "It's not always fair, sometimes you just have to— Okay. Okay, Tahkamenon. I'm going to trust you, but if you want us to take on religion, I hope you have a lot more than a beautiful rainbow up your sleeve."

Russ called a while later. "Hey, what's up? Autumn said you called."

"Believe me. You don't even want to know."

"Is everyone all right?"

"Oh, we're fine. For now anyway. At least until the religious right gets their hands on my latest writing."

Russ laughed. "The religious right, huh? What have you done now?"

"Just trashing the Ten Commandments. You know, saying that religion is weakening our faith."

"Oh. Is that all?"

"Shut up. You ought to see it on paper. Believe me, I'm waiting for someone to burn a cross on my lawn."

"Yeah? Well, you might want to go on out and clear any loose leaves or small twigs," Russ said, finding humor in my pain.

"You might want to go to hell," I responded more sharply than I had intended.

"Obviously not before you get there," Russ replied.

"Stop it. I can't help what I wrote. I'm going to tell everyone that you wrote this part anyway." I paused for a moment, collecting my thoughts. "Isn't religion supposed to save us?"

Russ took a minute to answer. "Ever hear of the Inquisition?" he asked in response. "Or what about the Middle East? Or what about—"

"I know. I get your point," I interrupted, my mind reeling with images. "But religion harmful? Isn't that a bit dramatic?" I was searching for a way to make the message less painful. I wanted only the peace not the destruction.

"Is it true—what you've written?" Russ asked.

"Absolutely," I responded.

"Well. There you go."

"No," I said, pausing for a moment. "Here *we* go."

"Oh yeah. I forgot that part. For better or for worse," Russ said, his voice strong and focused, "Here we go."

It was a simple statement, an unmistakable pledge. Much like our encounter in the St. Louis airport, it cemented our commitment, both to the message and to each other. It was another of our many points of no return. After I promised to fax him the writing the first thing Monday morning, I hung up the phone and tried to put the writing out of my mind. I wanted to focus on my family, on our Sunday. I wanted to feel normal. I wanted to understand what was happening. And why.

The message was not just beautiful. It was frightening. It was becoming more than I had bargained for. Yet even with the pain, even with my fear, I was drawn by the authenticity. No matter my rational reaction, my soul embraced each word. No matter my apprehension, my heart warmed with each newly discovered connection.

"Courage," I thought later that evening, my mind wandering back to the cryptic message of a few weeks ago. So it's courage that you want.

"Congratulations, Tahkamenon," I thought, in a brief moment of bravery. "If it's courage you're looking for, then you've come to the right place."

Chapter Nine

As Russ and I discussed the writing and the impact of the words, new barriers and new fears seemed to burst into view. Everywhere we turned, we faced more obstacles. We had come to expect them from the government, but they now seemed to infiltrate our lives. We saw barriers that we had resisted and those that we had fostered. We discovered barriers in our relationships, barriers within our hearts. Everywhere there were obstacles that we had never questioned, those that we had lived with and never truly seen.

As we questioned our own walls, the writing followed our thoughts.

> If there is a purpose to walls, it is to provide order, a basis for reference, an ability in the physical world to comprehend what otherwise remains unseen. And if walls do have purpose, how then do you restrain them from falling in upon themselves? From holding you in? From squelching the light?

How do you stop the flow of bricks and the habit of mortar? You must resist the satisfaction not only to build but also to strengthen, fortification that diminishes your soul. And what of walls that never meet? Do these have meaning or are they merely busywork in the hands of mankind?

As we looked around at our world full of walls, we continued to write of the burden, we continued to feel the weight of our own confinement. Each new passage that dealt with the barriers brought a sense of trepidation followed by a renewed feeling of hope. It was frightening to see the obstacles. It was exhilarating to trust in our ability to overcome them.

What tragedy your human bonds. What beauty. Distinction and limitation, sensual and confining. Suddenly you recognize the pull of parallel worlds as you struggle with the greater meaning of existence amid the toil and mundane moments of your life.

And the words continued. In many ways they were distressing, as truth often is, questioning our divisions, our distinctions, our values, and most importantly, our fear.

That which speaks to the heart, sings to the soul, and breaches the barriers of gender and race.

Distinctions of color are irrelevant. You are of one source. You are of one spirit. There is no black spirit, white spirit, yellow spirit, red spirit. There is one spirit that vibrates with all of the colors in harmony. Your color is merely the fragmentation of the reflection of the source that manifests in the physical form.

You have falsely infused meaning in the color of your skin, forgetting that your physical form is but an encasement, a limitation. Your skin can hold no true meaning.

It is a distinction that does not stand the test of the heart. In love, the distinction is meaningless.

The history of slavery is but a moment in the spirit. Release the fear. Release the hatred. Truth harbors no confinement. Have faith in the source and in your place within the whole.

No one can enslave you, for you are not your physical form. Your spirit cannot be restrained except by your own fear and lack of faith. You restrain yourself with hatred, with bitterness. There is no hate in love. There is no fear in faith. Tear down the walls. They were but a reaction. Allow yourself to stand in the light and this distinction will hold no meaning. It is a choice that you make. It is a path that has made you weary.

Hold my hand. Look into my heart. Allow yourself to know my soul. All is equal in the spirit. Just as rules instill fear, so too do artificial distinctions and protections. Trust in your equality. If you rely upon distinctions, you drive out the faith. You cut off the light. In the shadow of reflection, your color or your age or your gender appears meaningful. Do not be distracted. They do not vibrate with the truth.

Look at those who surround you. Focus not on the distinction but on the connection. Understand the irrelevance of form. Learn to appreciate your differences from the perspective that no true difference exists. The spirit knows not division. You see yourselves as separate because of the fragmentation of the light against the barriers. Do not allow yourself to live an illusion.

"The history of slavery is but a moment in the spirit?" I asked when I showed Russ the writing. "That's going to really piss some people off."

"Not if they understand it," Russ answered. "Tahkamenon is only saying that we need to move past this bizarre fixation on the color of our skin. All of us. We need to move past the fear and past the hatred. Whatever made us think that our skin was meaningful anyway?"

"Who knows?" I replied. "We seem to look for meaning in the strangest of places."

"Maybe that's why we so rarely find it."

"No one can enslave you, for you are not your physical form," I read aloud to Russ. "I need to remember that. I always let others hold me back."

"We all should remember that," Russ added. "Regardless of our color. Or our fear."

We wrote more of the barriers that we had created, those that we never intended, those that we often failed to comprehend.

What have you created? You look to your accumulations of material wealth and ignore the simultaneous creation of poverty. Does not food create hunger, wealth create poverty, possessions create emptiness, rules create fear? With false significance, you have created a lack for things that have no inherent meaning. Your need for this accumulation has created much crime. It has fostered much fear, much anger, much hatred. It is a hunger that has blocked the faith. It has blocked the light.

You have created only barriers. You have built many walls. Yet in all that you have done, you have not altered the truth. You cannot value the truth until you cease to value the distortion. You must look past the reflections. You must focus on the source.

Sometimes the references to walls were literal, as with this passage that questioned our system of punishment and disturbed me a great deal.

There is no greater irony than your prisons. Barriers of steel to hold blockaded souls. No room for the light, a constant reminder of your fear. What are the crimes that you choose to punish? What do you cherish? Jailed for right or for wrong, what is the impact of each incarceration?

Here you have a breeding ground for hatred, a hotbed of fear. One day you will release the prisoners, physical beings removed from the flow, taught to value the insignificant. You meet them now, bitter at their lack, vengeful at their loss. You must find a way to tear down the walls. It is not a confinement but an embrace that will alter the vibrations, that will allow for the filtering of the light.

Or keep it the same. You will see. Can you build your prisons big enough, tough enough, to hold the accumulation of hatred?

I literally trembled as I wrote these words, my fear tangible in my movements. I quickly called Russ and read him the passage. "I can't take this," I said when I finished reading.

"Take what?" Russ asked.

"This. These words. These thoughts. They upset me. Don't they bother you?"

"Do you believe them?" Russ asked, ignoring my question.

"Of course," I responded. "I believe them, but I can't accept them. I mean this is crazy. Do you think we should release all our prisoners?"

"We release them every day," Russ said. "But I don't think that you have to worry. At the rate we keep building prisons, we're going to have prisoners for a long time to come."

"Somehow that's even more frightening."

As we worked through our confusion, we wrote more passages about confinement, evaluating the methods we use to constrain our movement and hold each other in check.

From what are you being protected with these rules of your race? From greed and from hatred, from assault and from fear? Yet where did each come from—the fear and the hate? What role did the rules play in the creation of each?

Rules teach you to move based upon false concepts. You do so not because you believe but because you are led. Rules tell you not to question but to follow, not to believe but to do. And each carries a sanction, each instills great fear.

At what price do you accept the rules of your humanity? At what consequence do you deny them?

Who among you has the ability to create the rules that define your truth? Have you thought on this? Rules created for protection or for greed or for power. They are reactions. They are man-made. If you are being coerced, should you not question the motives? Acceptance has little to do with rules. Truth has no need for coercion.

And what of those who have lived their lives immersed in the rules, bloated with illusions of power and importance? Will they not resist the movement? What of each of us who views the walls as familiar, who has come to believe in the power of our constraints, who has been taught to deny the stirrings of our hearts?

At first resistance may seem natural, but no one has power or strength or security that is based on rules and not on the truth. You are never completely deceived by your own illusions. Always you hear that voice, no matter how small, no matter how distant, that recognizes the illusion for what it is. And with the recognition comes the fear that others will see you for who you are and not for the illusion you have worked so hard to create.

Yes, there are those who will resist the movement, still overwhelmed by fear. But in the end, it is these same individuals who will experience the greatest relief. The struggle of the illusion no longer will be required. The fear of revelation no longer a constant companion. True power. True strength. Total acceptance.

Now you light your feet upon the path and the rules hold little meaning. You laugh at their irrelevance, their inappropriateness. They may have served as protection until you found your way. But that is past, and this is present. To move more freely, you must now shed the weight of the barriers, excess baggage upon your soul.

With time, with understanding, you will come to evaluate your constraints more clearly. You will see their inherent weakness. You will experience your inherent strength. Eventually you will learn to recognize joy and come to embrace the power of following your heart.

Through it all, through the passages of confinement, through the heaviness of the words, there was a belief that the walls could be transcended, that the barriers were ours to overcome.

Here we make a journey, focusing on the movement. A journey not to a place, but a moment, searching not a destination but an understanding.

What makes you ready? It is the sadness of awareness, the burden of knowledge, the weight of comprehension that so torments your soul that you are unable to remain at that place you have come to know as comfort, unable to accept the confines of the walls that for so long now have defined the borders, not only of your thoughts but also of your being.

Try for a moment to think past the walls, to glimpse past the barriers, to see into your heart. Find the courage to experience hope. You have the ability to recapture the light and transcend the pain. You need only believe truly in the beauty and significance of your soul.

In this moment, you recreate your life. You alter your course or choose to remain on the path that has brought you forward to this juncture. If you find the present painful, does not it indicate a need to find a new course? Or perhaps a very old one, one that elicits great joy.

A step you take to alter your course, a movement not necessarily linear in motion. How do you do this? Even as you recognize the walls as destructive, you are unsure how to remove them, how to eclipse the confinement, how to bask even briefly in the light. You ask for guidance, for a message, for a test. And yet you remain surrounded by the bricks, their weight so much more noticeable upon your soul.

Was it not better before you understood? You try to close your eyes but your thoughts refuse to submerge. You sing other songs, louder, with more clutter. But the simplicity and authenticity of the melody you are trying to mask is much stronger than the distractions of the others.

So the step you take is one that leads you into the wall, into your fear, thrown against the biting surface of the jagged clay. You shiver against the cold of the brick and despair at its impenetrable features. But a glimmer of light shines through, either from within or without, an understanding that the wall, no matter how formidable, is of your own making. You have constructed it and therefore have the knowledge to tear it down.

Nothing in the spirit is harmful. You have no need for the walls. Yet you are both human and spirit. I understand this. I respect it. You experience light in many beautiful ways. You can continue to do so and still find joy. It is not necessary that you no longer see the distractions, that you no longer enjoy the beauty and diversity of your world.

Do not be constrained by the rules of humanity, even those professed in the name of the spirit, if they do not test true close to your heart. You can transcend the walls. You can choose to follow your heart.

The answer is simply a matter of priority. It is solely a matter of belief.

Chapter Ten

While we tried to make sense of the passages, the battle with the government raged on. I spent a great deal of time in Washington, meeting with congressmen, senators, and their staffs. Day after day, week after week, I pounded the legislative pavement, pleading our case, documenting our successes, challenging the propaganda of the competition, and spinning a little of our own.

It was exhilarating and exhausting. I could breathe in the power as I walked the corridors, learned my way through the endless maze of hallways, and maneuvered past the gatekeepers who protect the time, energy, and reputations of those they were paid to serve. I sometimes had to fight off the giddiness and force myself not to get sucked in by the illusion of might.

Our government was nothing that I expected and everything that I expected. It was intense, hardworking, committed. It was wasteful, boastful, and devastatingly partisan. I came to the doors of Congress passionate about my issue, ready to prove our ability to provide health care to the uninsured and to disprove the allegations of risk. But nobody was listening. Of course they allowed me to talk, to present my case. They shook my hand and nodded their heads. But there was no time for the details. Instead, they were calculating the strength of those for and against the issue, searching through the banter for clues to new alliances and wary of any trap that would anger those already on their side.

What was the political risk? No matter the issue, no matter the merits, what could the opponents say in a ten-second sound bite that would torpedo the next campaign? True or false. Right or wrong. It would not matter. Once spoken, it could not be retracted. It would not be erased from the minds of the voters. The politicians could not be concerned with the details, because they knew from experience that the public had little patience for the facts.

The game was brutal, especially since I was unwilling to compromise my beliefs to win. It was a constant dance, the type and tempo changing without warning, leaving me always a step or two behind.

This day ended as most—running in high heels up the concrete walkways, weighted by my black leather briefcase brimming with documents no one had cared to review and weary from one more day filled with "we'll see what we can do." I hailed a cab, settled in on my way back to National Airport, and feared missing my 5:30 flight as the taxi driver navigated rush hour traffic. This flight was critical. The next was not until 7:00. If I missed this one, I would not be home in time to help bathe the children, read books, sing songs, and kiss them goodnight. With all of the disappointment of Washington fresh on my consciousness, the thought of this additional loss was almost too painful to bear.

Luckily, I made the flight, walking through security just as the boarding call blared from invisible overhead speakers. I flashed my boarding pass and followed the line of fellow passengers out of the building and onto one of the trolley cars waiting to deliver us to the plane. I took a seat at the front of the second car, placing my briefcase close to my feet so that others could pass as they filled the remaining seats. I usually noticed little as they filtered by, overwhelmed by a day of studying every movement and expression of my audience, constantly trying to gauge if I was winning or losing support.

Tonight was different. One man caught my attention. His size was intimidating, and I pulled my briefcase even closer out of his way. I watched him closely, intrigued by his movement and appearance. His gait was labored as he maneuvered to the rear seats. I wondered if he was disabled or merely as tired as I. His skin was so black that it almost shone blue. His clothes were bold and colorful, with heavy gold jewelry adorning his throat and his wrist. With little more than an addition here or an adjustment there, he would have been clownish. As it was, he commanded respect. I stole a few more glances at him before I laid my head back against the side of the trolley and prayed that the forty-five minute trip home would go quickly.

Once out on the tarmac, I exited the trolley and ascended the rickety metal staircase to the plane. I had decided to write, to go far away from a day filled with power and politics, to find solace, I hoped, in the flow of the words. Once seated near the window, I reached down for my notebook and dug through my briefcase for a pen.

The man from the trolley took the seat next to mine. It was a small plane, with only two seats on each side of the aisle. I tried to adjust my position and sit back up into place as his size pinned me against the side. He surprised me with his lack of acknowledgment, not the usual smile or a nod of his head, only his immense and intriguing presence crowding my already inadequate space.

Fighting the panic of claustrophobia rising in my chest as the plane taxied and lifted, I managed to pull down the seat tray and began to write. Thankfully, the words flowed as I had come to trust that they would, without hesitation or conscious consideration.

The barriers of the physical world reflect the beauty of the spirit. But reflection allows room for distortion, allows space for doubt. You cannot have true faith in a reflection. No matter the clarity of the picture, it does not vibrate with the power of the truth.

So the answers to the questions of humanity lie not in this plane of reflections but in another—in the unity of the spirit that exists outside of your being and integrates within your soul.

The physical world holds many great adventures. It is an altered state of being, an hallucinogenic state that has hypnotized you with its visions and sensations, requiring higher and higher doses to support the illusion. Hence, you abuse the earth, sucking its nutrients with great addiction.

You are now entering a collective state of withdrawal. Illusions provide no nourishment to the soul. Addictions are of one source. They may manifest as physical but they originate from your lack of acceptance of the spiritual world. No one who basks in the light, unrestrained by the barriers, would ever seek illusion.

There is no point beyond perfection. There can be no true motivation for self-deception.

In your physical form, you reflect all that is good and bad in humanity. You must stop reflecting and be. You must stop reacting and act. Your failure in the physical plane has been a failure to test the veracity of your path.

Take my hand. I cannot show you perfection but I can show you the way. The length of the journey is immaterial. The energy of the path will carry us as far as we need to travel. It is this distinction that signifies the truth. The road will not make you weary. The further you move, the less nourishment you will require. The addiction can be broken. Each step weakens the walls and strengthens the structure.

Do not fear the destruction of the walls. Believe in the flow of the light. You do not have to create it. You do not have to find it. You need only allow it entry. The more free the movement, the more complete the transformation.

You journey not to the truth, for the truth surrounds you. You journey to acceptance—a journey of faith. It is not immersion, for you are already immersed in the truth. It is finding the faith to take a deep breath, to sink to the depths of the water unrestricted, and allow it to penetrate your being, to flow through your organs, to believe in its ability to sustain.

It is an old song with the startling ability to transform. There are many who acknowledge the message. Do not focus on the messenger. Resist the distraction. You need not learn; you need only understand.

Together we are but one voice, but one messenger. Truth is not acquired. It is innate. It is absolute. It is inside and outside of your physical form. It exists in totality but is revealed in degrees, allowing for the limitations of this plane, luring you to the other side.

Truth exists in the light as well as in the darkness but not in the shadows. It can only be represented in a reflection. It cannot be known. But a reflection of great quality can entice you to know more. A reflection is a lamp that lights the path. It is neither journey nor destination.

Illumination is reflection. Light in its truest form is vibration. Only in this form can you experience its energy.

Have faith. Truth exists within your being. Remove the walls and let it flow. The truth was not taken from you. You were given many distractions and allowed the choice to see or not to see. Once the doubt had entered, the rest was inevitable.

The words were flowing smoothly until a high-pitched sound filled my senses and drowned out the words. I looked around the cabin. No one else seemed to notice the noise. I focused carefully on the sound. It was eerie and beautiful. I shifted in my seat, barely able to move because of the size of the man beside me. And then I realized—it was coming from him. He seemed to be chanting, and the sound grew louder and louder. I looked around again. How could no one else notice?

I turned back to my writing, but it was impossible with this noise. I stole glances at the man from the corner of my eye. His lips were not moving, but his throat quivered slightly. "This is crazy," I thought, looking again around the cabin. "Why isn't anyone else looking at him?"

Then I noticed his hands. He held them on an open book in his lap, a religious book I was certain. It looked like a bible bound in tattered leather. The pages were of similar thin paper with golden edges. But the writing was in a foreign language. It looked Arabic, or at least what I imagined Arabic looked like. There was handwriting scribbled all over in the margins, and he was rubbing his big, fleshy hands over the words.

I turned to look at him more fully, growing more and more uncomfortable every moment. His eyes were closed. "What is he doing?" I wondered. His hands caressed the thin, yellowed pages. The music continued, a mix of chanting and humming. "Maybe this is like a dog whistle thing," I thought, trying to understand why everyone in the plane was not turning and looking for the source of the melody.

Frustrated and confused, I went back to my writing.

I cannot tell you the message. I can only beseech you to remove the barriers, tear down the walls, have faith, and fall within the flow. Immerse yourself in the healing, energizing forces of water and light.

"Look, if you can't tell me the message, how about if you just leave me the hell alone?" I thought. "It's not like I don't already have a million other things to do. I don't have time for these games." Oh God. Now I was talking back to Tahkamenon. I sunk my head into my free hand and rubbed my eyes. "I'm going to kill Russ," I thought before continuing to write.

Now as always, you find your way back by choosing faith over fear, love over hate, acceptance over attack or avoidance.

The sound intensified, making it impossible to concentrate on the writing. I closed my notebook and maneuvered to tuck it into my briefcase under the seat. The man beside me kept chanting, both the noise and his presence were suffocating. I shut my eyes and leaned back into the seat. My mind filled with thoughts of water and light and vibrations and walls. Common themes that had emerged from the writing. Common, but not yet understandable. And under it all, an unmistakable beauty. It was so hard to reconcile. Like this sound that seemed even louder in the darkness, strange, yet familiar, tormenting my mind and massaging my soul.

Once we landed, I hurried through the airport, exhausted and desperately wanting to be home. I stopped once at the end of the long corridor, looking back through the scattered sea of travelers. He wasn't there.

"That's okay," I thought. "I don't know why I'm looking for him anyway."

Later that night, Russ called to see how things had gone in Washington. He was intrigued by these trips, much more so than I. Of course he didn't have to face the disillusionment first hand, so I could understand his fascination. Anyway it was fun to drop names and tell him all about the latest power plays and strategies.

"How'd it go?"

"Oh, you know, 'we'll see what we can do.'"

"That bad, huh?" Russ groaned. "Don't these people understand you're trying to offer health-care coverage to the uninsured?"

"Sure they understand," I answered, sinking deep into my sofa. "It's not that they don't understand. It's that they don't care."

"But that's all I ever hear about. 'Cover the uninsured. We need to cover the uninsured.'"

"And from that you think they really want to *do* something?"

"Oh, sorry," Russ laughed. "I lost my head for a moment. I forgot that this is Washington we're talking about."

"I forgive you. I'd forget it was Washington myself if I didn't need their help so urgently."

"You sound beat," Russ said softly.

"I am. You wouldn't believe my flight back."

"Lots of turbulence?"

"No. Just high-pitched chanting."

"Chanting? What? Did you fly back with the Hare Krishna convention or something?"

"No, just one incredibly large black man who sat beside me, chanting the whole way home."

"No way. What did everyone else do?"

"Nothing. Apparently I'm the only one who heard him."

"Really?" Russ asked. "What happened?"

I told Russ all about watching the man board the shuttle, about the richness of his skin, about the oppression of his size as he pressed into the seat beside me. I explained I had been writing until interrupted by the sound. How I didn't understand at first where it had come from, but now I was certain that it was this man. I described the worn leather book with the foreign writing and how he gently rubbed the page with his eyes closed.

"Was he blind?" Russ asked.

"I don't think so. I thought that maybe at first when he rubbed the pages. But they had handwriting all over them, and nothing appeared to be raised."

Russ was quiet for a moment. I was more than ready to say good night and go to bed.

"He was an angel," Russ said.

I was instantly annoyed. Russ drove me insane with these crazy statements. "What the hell are you talking about?" I asked.

"Don't you get it? The chanting that no else could hear, the book he read without seeing—he's an angel. A big, black, beautiful angel."

"You're crazy. He wasn't an angel," I said, my voice rising. "He didn't even look like an angel."

Brian, sitting beside me on the couch and watching television, turned and looked at me. "Who's not an angel?" he asked.

"Don't worry," I answered. "It's just Russ being Russ."

"What do you mean 'Russ being Russ'?" Russ demanded. "And if you're so smart, what does an angel look like anyway?"

"I don't know—angelic."

"Oh well, there's an answer for you," Russ said laughing. "You can tell you've just spent the whole day in Washington."

"Fine Russ. He was an angel. Come to think of it, I even think I saw a halo. Can I go to bed now?"

"No you can't go to bed, and stop being so sarcastic. You just had an encounter with an angel—a big, black, beautiful angel. Doesn't that tell you something?"

"It tells me that we're both losing our minds."

"It tells me that we both are blessed." Russ paused and then added, "Especially you. I can't believe you get an angel."

"Don't be jealous. I promise, I'll share."

"Funny. I don't think you have much of a choice."

"Look," I said, barely able to stay awake, "my angel wore me out. He was noisy and took up too much room. Can I please go to bed now?"

"Sweet dreams," Russ replied. "Maybe your angel will come to visit you?"

"More likely the men with the white coats."

"You're such a skeptic. Why didn't Tahkamenon send me the angel? It's totally wasted on you."

"Good night, Russ."

"Good night, Pumpkin."

"Russ," I said before he had a chance to hang up.

"Yes?"

"Do you think this means that God forgives me for what I wrote about religion?"

"I think it means that He wrote it himself."

"Oh that makes sense," I responded. "Then why don't you tell me this—if I'm flying with angels and writing God's words, why can't I even get a stupid piece of legislation passed?" I was very tired and sorry I hadn't gotten off of the phone when I had had the chance.

"Maybe the legislation is just not meant to be," Russ responded. "It makes sense to me."

I didn't have the strength to argue. "Good. Just so long as it makes sense to one of us." I said good-bye again, hung up the phone, massaged my temples, and turned to Brian. "Remind me never to talk to him after nine o'clock. It hurts my brain." Brian rubbed my leg, too engrossed by the television to respond. I leaned over and kissed him. "Look I'm beat. I'm going up to bed."

"Huh? Oh, okay. I'll be up just as soon as this is over." Brian briefly tore his eyes away from the set. "Hey, who's the angel?"

"Oh just a big, black angel who came back with me on the plane," I replied rolling my eyes.

"Coming from Washington?" Brian said with a smile. "I doubt it."

"Good point," I thought. "I wish I would have thought to say that to Russ."

I went upstairs, undressed, crawled into my bed, and opened my notebook to read what I had written on the plane. Even though I was exhausted, I wanted to write more, so I flipped to the back and released the words.

How long have you known me? An answer hard to relay in human terms. I ask when did you not know me? Were you surprised when you found me waiting just outside your door?

You seem confused with your own answers. Break free of linear thought. We have known each other in several dimensions. Our connection is eternal, yet we each remain distinct. At times you have been more focused on the connection, at others on the distinctness. But my ability to startle you is quite limited. You know my thoughts before I express them, for I speak only with love.

We have never been strangers. Is that enough of an answer for now? In case you are wondering, we never will be.

"I've never been strangers with whom?" I wondered, reading the words with a great deal of confusion. "Tahkamenon? The angel? Oh God, now Russ has me calling him an angel. I'm too tired to deal with this." I closed the notebook, turned off the light, and collapsed.

The bed and the darkness comforted me as I let the world slip away from my consciousness. "What if he was an angel?" I thought, hating Russ intensely. "No, no. Please let me sleep," I answered. I rolled over in bed and put my pillow over my head, my mind splitting into divergent camps.

"He could have been."

"He wasn't."

"How do you know?"

"I don't—"

"Exactly."

I pulled the pillow down and opened my eyes. "Okay,

okay. So he was an angel." My mind settled at the acceptance. "Wow, an angel." I curled up peacefully on my side. "An angel is cool," I thought. "God knows, the way things have been going with the government, I certainly could use one."

"Thanks, Tahkamenon," I whispered into the darkness as I drifted off to sleep. "This is even better than a rainbow."

Chapter Eleven

My name is Tahkamenon. I knew you once long ago. I know your heart, your soul, your intentions. I come to you anticipating that together we can know the hearts of millions.

There is much to be done. Russ has brought us together. He is the glue. He illuminates the possibilities. I allow you to write, to use your gift, to translate the meaning I impart. Russ is able to hear me. That is his gift. With his voices he can speak for many. You need to encourage him. To let him see his abilities and trust in their impact.

You share a common goal. Love has brought you together. Neither saw it alone. Neither quite understood. Together you are beginning to understand. You are walking through the fields of flowers, experiencing their color, feeling their vibrations, lost in the dizziness of their aroma. Hand in hand, you are approaching the water, acknowledging the reflection for what it is and for what it is not. Both are important, an integral part of what you need to dispense.

Others will understand. Trust this. Have faith. Allow yourself to speak directly to their souls, uninhibited by knowledge, breaking the barrier of the intellect. The truth I bring is contagious. You must feel it first. You must accept completely. You are moving. I see it in your words. I feel it in your heart, your soul ablaze with the radiant fire of your belief.

I love you. You are as my child and my friend. I am here to protect and encourage you. You hold the wisdom that you wish to impart within you. I come only to open the door. Russ will help also. He understands the darkness within you. It is the same as that within himself. I understand your light. I see you both for your beauty, your potential.

Sing your song. It is a beautiful voice, a meaningful message. It is truth revealed in degrees so that you are able to absorb and describe.

Your life is your own to live, even through the connections, even with the unity. There are individual realities and mass realities. Both exist simultaneously. Both are altered by your thoughts and by your actions. The physical plane allows you the opportunity to fully experience yourself, to align your own actions with your own thoughts before you are able to enter the greater reality of unity.

You have the ability to alter your path, to change your life. And once you have chosen to do so in a manner that brings your actions into alignment with your higher purpose, you will see a realm of possibilities previously undisclosed.

You have purpose inherent in your being. Both individual purpose and collective purpose, but you must accept that which is yours alone before you can truly expand on our collective journey.

I come because I trust in your ability and your intent to bring the message to others. I have watched as you have touched them, as you have opened their hearts with your love.

For now you have come to recognize each other, but there are many, many more. You will know them soon, in this plane or the next, and you will recognize each also as your friend.

Remember always that I love you. It is a great journey upon which we embark.

My mind and emotions reeled from the impact of the words. In one incredible flow, Tahkamenon reached out to me directly, discussing why me, why Russ, why the message. My breath held tight in my chest and the world slipped away as I focused fully on the passage, the words washing over me in wave after wave of significance.

After months of questioning my involvement, the answer seemed so clear—because he loved me, because he trusted me, because he believed in my intentions, because he knew the contents of my heart. And the relationship with Russ was destined. We needed each other. Tahkamenon wanted us both.

I had been questioning the role of destiny, and now it took on a whole new meaning. "You have individual purpose and collective purpose inherent in your being." Of course that was the answer. I was not powerless to direct my life and yet there remained an overall plan, an eternal flow. I could work with it or against it. I could find happiness or pain.

Luckily, Russ and I had chosen the course that led us into each other's life. The battle with the government had drawn us together. We had chosen to act with integrity, to stay true to ourselves in the face of adversity. The government may have been winning the fight, but we alone were holding fast to our souls.

I read the words again, covered in their love, surrounded by their beauty, immersed in their warmth. I kept coming back to those powerful words: "I love you. You are as my child and my friend." Many people loved me, deeply, beautifully, but always humanly. This was love from my soul. It carried no barriers. It not only touched me but also absorbed me in its caress. The words lifted me higher than I had ever imagined and left me totally unprepared for the fall.

But the fall came. For within this passage full of love and encouragement was the responsibility of reaching out to others, of opening their hearts to the voice of their souls. "Tahkamenon," I pleaded. "Please, please don't ask. I'm not strong enough. I'm too battered by my job. I'm too overwhelmed by my life." Tears welled in my eyes and streamed silently down my face. "I love you. I would do anything, anything that I could, but I can't—"

"Then do this," came the voice in my head. It was strong and compassionate, immediate and eternal. It was, without a doubt, the voice of Tahkamenon.

"I want to. Whatever you want. Whatever you need. But you need a leader. You need a celebrity. You need someone that people will listen to."

"They will listen to you, you and Russ. Trust this. Have faith."

"Please stop," I begged. "I'm not strong enough. I'm too confused to explain. I'm all used up. I have nothing left to give."

"You have everything. You have your heart. You have your soul."

I covered my ears out of habit, trying to stop the sound in my head. I realized then that my eyes were closed, and I opened them quickly, wanting the voice to disappear. It did, but its impact remained. For there, in front of my eyes, were the words on the paper, commanding me to action, asking for something that I was unprepared to give.

The love now was painful. How could I disappoint someone who loved me so completely? Still I could not do what he had asked. It was too big. It was too much. Maybe he was divine, but somehow he was also confused. He had found the wrong person. He had opened the wrong heart.

I chose not to tell Russ about the passage. I hated the deception, but it was the only way. He wouldn't understand. He would see only the love and ignore the impossibility of the request. He would take the goodness and fail to understand that I saw the responsibility. He would want to take this further. I wanted the words to go away.

But not Tahkamenon. I could not go that far. I wanted him to be silent, but I desperately needed him to stay. As much as I knew that I could not do his bidding, I understood also that I could never relinquish my soul.

I was nervous talking with Russ. How to speak and hide my heart? He spoke of Tahkamenon. I pretended to be distracted by my work. The pressure from the government had become so intense that it provided a convenient cover for the sudden break in my writing, for the lack of enthusiasm in my response.

Everything was changing. I tried to reenter my life as I had left it months before, before the discovery of our connection, before the creation of these assorted and significant words. But that was impossible. I now saw the walls. I now felt the doubt. I now knew in my heart that there was a better place and feared that I had neither the courage nor the strength to find it.

Afraid to reach for the light, I fell into my humanness and sank uncontrollably into the depths of my fear.

Chapter Twelve

The depression was devastating. It wiped out my sense of taste, my sense of color, my sense of depth, my sense of humor. Everything looked and felt flat and dingy. Through the shadows of my eyes, the walls of our new home were gray and crumbling. I dreaded eating dinner as much as cooking it. The pictures on the television appeared as paper cutouts, both the figures and the words void of animation.

I observed these changes as if I were reading about them, following but not really participating. I wanted to run without knowing to where. I kept thinking of driving to the West Coast, getting on a ship and sailing off into the horizon. I did not even want to set sail from the East Coast where I lived. It had to be further. I wanted to be so very, very far away. I felt myself disconnecting from everything and everyone, floating away into nothingness.

The moments of inspiration faded. I could still write pieces but not the flowing pages of beauty on which I had come to rely. And the writing was darker, much more cognizant of the confinement of our world.

In this space I have grown weary, weighted by the
emptiness, worn from the years of supporting the walls.
It is both dark and familiar, restraining my movement,

withholding my soul. I look at the bricks and wonder aloud that this is not what was intended, this confinement, this loneliness.

So many lines. So many limits.

No one seemed to notice this devastating change. Or they noticed the small things—like I wasn't smiling or I wasn't talking. No one noticed that I was desperate. No one noticed that I was dying.

I was so tired. This was something tangible, something I could recognize, something that I could say. So I said it over and over, "I'm really tired. I'm sorry. What did you say? I wasn't listening. I'm so tired. I'm so very, very tired."

"You've got to slow down," everyone responded. "Of course you're tired. Who wouldn't be? Your family, the company, the lawsuit—something has got to give."

And it did. I'm not sure what it was, but it felt a great deal like my soul. I was lost in a wild sea of commotion, unable to find a familiar rock or sandy ridge to catch my footing. I reached for Brian, but he failed to see my outstretched arms. Depression was something that he did not seem to understand.

I had been telling him that I was tired, overwhelmed, apprehensive for two years as I battled with the government. I had no new words to describe this new feeling. And Brian did not perceive the horrible change in meaning that the old ones now held. I was upset with him for not understanding. "How can he pretend to love me?" I thought. "He doesn't even see me."

I began to focus the weight of all of this darkness on Brian. Every moment he spent at work, every ounce of his energy not directed at me, became further proof of his lack of concern. I was angry, incredibly and inexplicably angry.

The anger welled and exploded, the only emotion seemingly strong enough to overcome my despair.

"Get out," I yelled one fateful Sunday morning, shaking with fury and fear.

"What?" Brian asked, tilting his head, his mouth half open in dismay.

"Get out," I repeated. "It's over. I can't live like this any longer." The words raced from my body, my voice trembling with every word.

Brain stared into my eyes but did not approach me. He seemed to be measuring my movements as much as my words.

"You heard me," I snapped, tears spilling down my cheeks. "It's over. Get out. I can't keep living this lie."

Brian's voice now trembled in response to my own. "What lie, Valerie? What the hell are you talking about?"

"Our lie Brian," I shouted. "You know—the one that you love me." Even I had to pause at this statement, but once voiced, there was no turning back.

Brian came toward me, his face flushing. "What do you mean? Of course I love you." I froze in my chair unable to bear his closeness even as I wanted nothing more than to get up and throw myself into his embrace. He reached for me. I hit his arm.

"What the hell is wrong with you?" he yelled, pulling his arm back to the protection of his body.

"Everything," I replied, wiping the tears from my face. "Everything I've lived for is over."

"Jesus, Valerie. You're not making any sense." Brian lowered his voice and reached for me again.

I stood and broke away from his grasp. If he held me, I would collapse. I would fall completely into the despair that surrounded me. I now truly believed that he didn't love me. "How could he?" I thought. "What is there to love?"

Caught up in the moment, I turned back around to face him, my voice suddenly calm. "Look, we can do this. I know it will be difficult on the kids. I'm sorry for that, but they'll survive. We both did."

The reference to the divorces we both endured as children was so hurtful, especially in this context, especially as we discussed repeating the pattern of pain. Everything hurt. My heart disintegrated as I thought of telling the children, of telling our mothers, of telling our friends. Brain's face was contorted. His stare was blank. And still I went on. "I'll stay in the house at first. We'll split up all the stuff." I said, waving my arm in disgust at the contents of our home. "And the bills. The kids will stay with me, but you can see them whenever you like. This is not about them. You're a great father."

My eyes dried as I hashed out the details. Brian's flooded as I spoke of the children, as I laid out our new life in dirty detail.

"You're really serious, aren't you?" Brian asked in amazement.

"Dead serious," I flatly responded.

"How can you even possibly think that I don't love you?"

"How can you even possibly think that you do?"

Brian sat on the couch and took a deep breath. "Please sit down," he begged.

I did, but not close. I could not bear the thought of his touch. My mind swirled. "Oh my God, what am I doing? What if he really leaves?" I asked myself. My heart sank even further as I saw through the details, as I imagined the days and the nights without his presence, as I imagined my life without his love.

Still I could not stop. The argument now had life of its own. I mouthed the hateful words and felt their sting deeply. I had lost control in anger before. But never like this. Never this far. And Brian seemed different as well, unsure how to react or what to say. Usually when I got mad and said crazy things, Brian focused on calming me down. His parents had been counselors and teachers. He had been raised with their skills, bred with their compassion.

But now he was hurt, hurt too fully to focus on my feelings. He looked as if he had never before seen me, as if a stranger had walked into the room and started tearing his world apart.

This I took as a further sign that he did not truly know me, that he could not possibly love me. I ignored the fact that I could not even recognize myself, and hated him for deceiving me, for pretending to love me, for luring me into his heart. I was determined to break free before I could be hurt any further. The thought of the children tortured me. Even as I was running from Brian, I knew I could not run from them. Here I could not reconcile my feelings so I refocused on Brian, determined to finish this confrontation and retreat into the comfort of my own desperation.

The pause in my yelling had given Brian a moment to compose himself. "I do love you," he said, reaching over and rubbing my leg gently. My skin burned at his touch. "I didn't know that you were so unhappy." He looked down into his lap. "I didn't know that I made you so unhappy." His voice cracked and his body shook with tears.

My heart broke, the snap drowning my senses. I wanted to hold him more than anything. I wanted to ask him to hold me back. I wanted to tell him that this wasn't his fault. But nothing seemed more impossible, nothing less invincible than the wall I had masterfully erected in the growing space between us.

I leapt from the couch and ran upstairs, stopping only long enough to grab a handful of Kleenex from the bathroom counter. Ashleigh looked at me with concern as I passed the door to the playroom where she sat playing a game with her brothers.

"I'm just tired," I managed to say, hurrying to my room and closing the door behind me. I headed toward our bathroom but got only as far as the closet, a large walk-in filled with business suits and polo shirts. I shut the closet door softly, sinking between my dresses, wanting only to disappear.

It was then, slumped deep within the fabric, that I felt something sticky catch on my skin. Dry cleaner bags. I ran my hand up and down two plastic wrapped dresses. I maneuvered in between them, not consciously thinking any further ahead.

Slowly I caressed the plastic, pulling it from the dresses, wrapping my body from each side. I was not thinking of death exactly. Only escape. I had no place else to run. I held the plastic snug around my shoulders. I closed my eyes and imagined surrounding my face, blocking my breath, stopping my pain.

I heard my youngest son in the distance, muffled through the walls, "Mommy. Mommy, Eric hit me."

I cried uncontrollably. I held the plastic in place but could not move it further. I sank into the darkness, crying so hard that I did not ever bother to slow the sobs or wipe away the tears. Eventually I collapsed, curled up amidst old shoes and purses and other discarded remnants of what used to be my life.

I'm not sure how long I lay there. I woke to Brian's voice and his hand on my shoulder. "Wake up, Valerie," he whispered. I tried but my eyes were so swollen that they would hardly budge. When I did manage to look up, I saw that his were red and swollen as well.

"What time is it?" I asked.

"About two." Brian stared at the wall above me. "The kids want to go swimming. We promised them yesterday."

Before I could respond, I thought of the plastic. I was intensely embarrassed and did not want Brian to see. Luckily, it had slipped from my hands as I slept, lying in piles on the floor, apparently posing no danger. "Okay. Okay," I said, shutting my eyes and trying to regain my composure. "Are they okay?" I asked.

"I think so," Brian answered. "Ashleigh seems concerned, but I don't think the boys have noticed anything. They're much too busy beating on each other."

I looked at Brian and smiled slightly. "It's just a sign of affection."

"Maybe today has just been too affectionate all around," Brian responded, avoiding my gaze.

His sarcasm stung me, but I had no strength to reply. I followed him out of the closet. We silently changed into our bathing suits and gathered the towels. We headed for the YMCA, and the kids revived me in a way that only kids can do. It was hard not to get caught up in their excitement. Brian and I put our earlier discussion on hold. The children would have this one afternoon at least. I wondered if it would be our last. I wondered if Brian was wondering that as well.

The indoor pool was wonderful, refreshing, a welcome distraction to the dreariness of February. I held Alex in my arms as Brian played with Ashleigh and Eric, teaching them to turn back flips in the water. I admired his spirit. I loved my children. When Brian took Alex to give me a break, I only thought briefly of sinking to the bottom and never coming up.

The next several weeks were hell. I broke down at my office and was forced to seek help. Realizing that my thoughts were not rational, Brian and I called a tentative truce. We coexisted in limbo, each hoping that the tension would eventually break.

From the depths of my desperation, from an emptiness that I had never before experienced, from a darkness that consumed my life, I began again to write. And once I started, the words flowed so quickly that I had to race to keep up. My mind unable to process the next line until it fell on the paper, my thoughts unknown until they formed fully in black and white.

We smiled as we built the wall, that first one in the garden. Mightily we handled each brick, relishing its weight, admiring its texture. We spread the mortar briskly, allowing the coolness to ooze between our fingers. And brick after brick we continued the movement, lulled by the repetition, consumed with our pride.

We had heard of other gardens where walls had been erected. It was necessary to define the limits and restrict the entry. For the garden was beautiful, tranquil, serene. Without a wall, it may be ruined. Without a wall, there would be no control. If we did not build, then surely someone else would, someone who may seek to deny us entry. That was the deciding factor, the final call to action.

The decision made, we worked tirelessly to ensure the wall sufficient, the barrier complete. Feeling confined at first, we built a door to permit us choice. Rejoicing in our accomplishment, we collapsed onto the lushness of the garden floor, secure behind our fortress, happy within our walls, and drifted off to sleep.

We awoke to much commotion, the sound of fists upon the door. Quickly we pulled the door open. "Do not worry," we said. "We did this only for your protection, to keep the garden sacred, to keep the garden safe."

For many days and many nights, we allowed the door to open freely until that day when the heretics came and questioned our authority, our right to encircle the garden with walls. Immediately we gathered the believers. "These are those we warned you about," we said with much conviction. "They are here to disturb your peace."

The believers voted quickly to evict the heretics, relishing the feeling of power, their chance to keep the garden pure. They rallied by our side and expelled the opposition. They smiled with satisfaction. We smiled back with great relief.

In time we sensed uneasiness, disquiet in the garden. We heard murmurs where before there had been only singing. A plot, we thought, to challenge our authority. We had heard of this happening before in other gardens, surrounded by other walls. So we ordered the erection of new barriers, further insulation for the garden, further protection for ourselves.

Some questioned the impact of the barriers—more heretics in our midst. So we turned the others against them, encouraging those who would believe without question and follow without dissent. We praised these for their loyalty, their ability to see the evil in the others, their ability to ignore the evil in us.

And the deeper we went into the garden, the smaller we built the spaces, redefining worthiness with the placement of each brick. We relished the eviction of others, turning them out into the cold with a feeling not of sadness but relief.

Many walls were built and many needy were cast aside before the moment of realization that the walls had closed in upon us. Yet we continued to build, brick after brick, until we sat alone in the darkness, the beauty of the garden no longer ours to enjoy, the warmth of the sunshine unable to penetrate the coldness of the brick. We huddled in the shadows and wondered at those who had been denied entrance. If this were so terrible, imagine what misery must lie outside of the walls.

Then one day from beyond the fear shone a thought that maybe removing just one wall would allow some light, restore some warmth. The risk seemed insurmountable at first, until that day, until that moment, when the search for the light was no longer a choice but an act of desperation, a realization that there were no options, that we could no longer exist without hope.

So painfully, fearfully, we beat at the bricks and dug at the mortar until a ray of light appeared and warmed our hands and touched our hearts. And the fear subsided just a bit, coming in waves, paralyzing us at times but allowing us solace at others. We continued to remove the bricks, unaware that walls were falling, until we found ourselves in the midst of those whom we had cast aside.

They were bitter at first, still stinging from the pain of exclusion. But without the isolation, they had continued to grow. Jealous when they turned toward the wall, they had learned to look outward, to relish the warmth of their spaces, to enjoy the kinship of those in their midst. The light now shone clearly on the destruction that lie within the confines and protection of the space they had longed to fill, and they could no longer feel such hatred at the exclusion.

Once outside of our walls, we no longer pitied their existence but loathed the emptiness of our own.
In time, they led us to their walls, less distinct, less invincible. They took our hands and asked that we show

them the way to break down their barriers, to join those on the other side. Again the fear, the loss of security, but with faith, we removed more bricks. Together we transcended more walls.

With time the garden returned to its former beauty. Thankfully, in the warmth of the sunlight, we returned to our former selves.

I read the words and saw the faintest of glimmers. Where nothing else had succeeded, this writing was a much-needed message of hope. I reread the passage, holding it closely, desperately pulling at its light. My thoughts kept coming to rest on one pivotal line. "Until that day, until that moment, when the search for the light was no longer a choice but an act of desperation, a realization that there were no options, that we could no longer exist without hope."

"I understand that day," I thought, my mind rejoicing in the recognition. "I understand the desperation of that moment." And for the first time in well over a month, I understood the need for hope.

I spent a long time falling into depression. It took quite a while to climb back out of the darkness that had overtaken my life. The writing did not magically take away the pain. It did not bring color back to my world or taste back to my food. But it held out a ray of hope. It helped me to see the moment for what it was. It helped me to realize that there was a path to the light. As always it was my choice to walk upon it, a choice I could rightly describe as an act of desperation.

As with most things that I had learned from Tahkamenon, this message was both absolute and inadequate. The truth of the words was indisputable, but the application to my world was always imperfect at best. The cover never quite fit. At first I saw this as a defect in the message. I now believe that the fit is perfect, that it is our perception, our human perspective, that blocks this from our view.

Realizing my options, I chose to get better, to see a counselor, to take the medication that she explained would break my thoughts out of the negative patterns that months of stress and fear and apprehension had hardwired in my brain. My counselor viewed the battle with the regulators as the cause for my depression. I saw the logic but knew that the struggle was not only with the government. It remained first and always a battle within myself.

I shared the writing with Russ. He was silenced by its impact. I didn't push him. I had so much to contend with. I was desperately trying to find my way back.

A few days later, I arrived at my office to find a fax on my desk. The cover said only, "I hope this makes you smile." I flipped the page and quickly read what Russ had sent.

Think as you read this, deep within your soul, you devoutly wish to talk to him who will respond and who loves you and whom you have missed these many years. Call out to Tahkamenon in your own way, and he will respond in his. Cry out, not of fear but for love, the love you have not yet experienced yet know to be yours.

Love yourself and he will love you. Believe in yourself and others will believe.

Go into the sunlight. Pass beyond the walls to where you see the sun shining the brightest. Bathe in the warmth and lift your eyes skyward. Say your greeting and he will respond with his. You need only open the door. You need only tear down the walls. Fear little, for you cannot fear not at all. Not yet. Not here. Listen. Listen and you will hear the soft footsteps of an old friend back from a long journey. In time you will recognize the voice, and then at once the message will be clear.

This is the voice of peace you have heard forever. From far beyond the walls, from deep within your soul, it has spoken since the beginning of time. Judge not. Believe it so, for in the belief you will have stepped outside of your walls and experienced joy.

Tears spilled down my cheeks as I dialed the phone. "Thank you," I said as soon as Russ answered.

"Did it make you smile?"

"Even better. It made me cry."

"That's not better," Russ said. "You've been crying for a month."

"This is better. It's happy crying," I responded, my voice choked with emotion. "The writing is beautiful. It's perfect. 'This is the voice of peace you have heard forever.' What a wonderful description. A perfect fit."

We were quiet for a moment. "Are you going to be okay?" Russ asked.

"I think so," I said as convincingly as I could.

"You know that I love you," Russ said, more a comment than a question.

"I know," I answered.

"And Brian loves you."

"I know."

"And your children. And your family. And I could go on and on."

"And Tahkamenon," I responded. "Don't forget Tahkamenon."

"Definitely Tahkamenon," Russ added and laughed. "He loves you even when the rest of us find you impossible to understand."

"Hey, I thought you were cheering me up."

"I am. Don't I hear you smiling?"

"I refuse to answer on the grounds that it may incriminate me."

"There," Russ replied with conviction. "I rest my case."

Russ was right. I was blessed with incredible people who loved me in spite of all of the craziness, who saw my worth even when I did not. No matter the hatred of my words, Brian never left me, and I began to see him again for the man that he was—a man who loved me completely. And I was once again able to receive his love. It was not easy. Not for either of us. My words had hurt him deeply. So we had to walk together through the pain I had created. We had to find our way back into each other's heart.

I stopped the medication long before the counselor had anticipated. She feared a relapse. I knew in my heart that it would not happen. I knew in my soul that I had found hope. I emerged from the darkness stronger, with a better understanding of the confinement, with a deeper appreciation of the impact of the barriers.

The pain eased slowly but steadily. Looking back I now see even this pain as a gift. It allowed me to see the light more clearly. It allowed me to turn away from the darkness.

For all of the torment, for all of the desperation, it allowed me to choose to live.

Part Two

❖

The Message

Chapter Thirteen

"This is 100 percent publishable. The question now is what are you going to do about it?"

My heart jumped in my chest. "Oh my God. Oh my God. He said '100 percent publishable,'" I thought as I sat at the table, Russ at my side, Ruth O'Lill and Joe Dunn facing us. Two real writers. Both had been published. I met Ruth through my volunteer work with the Alzheimer's Association. She was an author and she introduced me to Joe, her husband, author of four books, Pulitzer Prize judge, managing editor of publications for Edgar Cayce's Association for Research and Enlightenment. And now here they sat, meeting Russ and me for lunch, Joe resting his hand on a bright blue folder containing our writing and voicing these unbelievable words.

I heard Russ suck in a breath. We didn't look at each other. We couldn't. We would scream or cry or lose all sense of control. "Focus, Valerie. Focus," I commanded, realizing that Joe's lips were still moving yet no sounds were penetrating the thunder in my head. Before I could speak, Russ stopped him. Thank heaven for Russ.

"Wait. Wait just a minute. Could we back up here?" Russ asked, holding up his hand like a traffic cop. "Could you please say that one more time?"

"Say what?" Joe asked, eyeing Russ wearily.

"You know, what you said about publishable," Russ responded. We all laughed. Not Russ. He was serious.

"I said it's 100 percent publishable. Now that doesn't mean—"

"No, wait," Russ interrupted. "I just want to stay with this for a moment."

I looked down at the table, dropping my head in my hands. "Why did I bring him?" I thought. "He's going to embarrass me. I know it. I just know it."

"Now when you say '100 percent,'" Russ continued in an accusatory tone, "that means that beyond any possible shadow of a doubt, not any doubt at all, the writing that you have in that folder," he paused long enough to point, "is definitely, positively, absolutely publishable. Is that what you mean?"

My temper flared. "Yes Russ, I believe that's what he said," I answered, hoping that Joe and Ruth were not offended by his tone.

"That *is* what I said," Joe responded. "Now that doesn't mean—"

"Wait," Russ again interrupted. "I have one more—"

"Russ! Would you shut up and let him finish his sentence?" I shrieked.

"Sure. No problem," Russ said, turning to look at me as if he had no idea why I was so upset.

"I was just trying to say that being publishable doesn't mean that it will be published," Joe said. "If you are willing to work for it, I think that you can do it. But it will be a hell of lot more like a marathon than a stroll in the park."

"We'll walk on our hands if we have to," Russ responded.

"What did you like about it?" I asked, unable to let the compliment rest. "Why do you think it's publishable!"

Joe opened the blue folder and quickly scanned several pages of random passages that we had written over the previous months. "It's beautiful," he replied.

"And so powerful," Ruth said.

I smiled. Those were our words. Russ and I had called the Tahkamenon writing many things over the last year, but it always came down to this—beautiful and powerful.

"Believe me," Joe continued, "I've read a lot of writing by a lot of writers. Many times I've read beautiful, lyrical poetry. But this is more. This is lyrical poetry with a message."

I was certain that I was going to be sick. I wanted to run but Russ had me blocked in my seat and the bathrooms were at the back of the restaurant. So I took a deep breath and willfully held the bile in my stomach in check. I noticed that Russ was holding his fork empty and in mid-air. "Good, pretend that you are eating," I thought. "Do something normal and maybe then they won't realize that we're complete lunatics."

Neither Ruth nor Joe seemed to notice our silliness. Or maybe they did notice and were compassionate enough to ignore it. They kept the conversation going in spite of our inability to properly respond to anything that they said. "Now Ruth says you *both* are writing this," Joe continued. "How does that work?"

"Oh God," I thought. "Here we go. The question I dread. Here's where we tell them that we're talking to dead people, and they politely excuse themselves and go back to work." Before I summoned the courage to answer, Russ jumped right in.

"Well it's kind of a long story," Russ replied, sounding much more like himself. "You see I've been talking to this spirit that I call Tahkamenon all of my life. And then Valerie had a visit from her dead father-in-law and—"

I grabbed Russ's leg, my chest tightening with panic. "No, don't say it that way," I screamed in my head, hoping beyond hope that he somehow would hear.

Russ glanced at me briefly and continued. "So she told me about that. And I told her about Tahkamenon. And I said that I would send her some writing. Only I didn't, or before I had a chance—"

"Had a chance?" I interjected. "I waited for two months."

Russ looked at me again and turned back to Ruth and Joe. "As I said, before I had a chance to send her my writing, she wrote the passage about Tahkamenon coming into my consciousness. It's there, in the folder." Russ relaxed back into the seat of the booth. "It was unbelievable. She described my experience exactly. It was then that I knew that she was talking to Tahkamenon too."

I watched both Ruth and Joe, scrutinizing their eyes, analyzing their gestures. I could not believe what I was seeing. They both had leaned forward, focusing fully on Russ, seemingly caught up in the story. No sign that they thought we were crazy, no indication that they were about to get up and leave.

"Only she didn't believe me," Russ continued.

"Who would?" I asked, holding up my hands and looking to Ruth and Joe for support. They laughed, and I continued. "I never heard Tahkamenon at first. I just wrote, and somehow I was writing as if I were Russ. I knew what he experienced. I felt it." I leaned forward across the table myself. "I still don't know if that means that I'm talking to Tahkamenon. But I do believe—"

"You still don't know if you're talking to Tahkamenon?" Russ asked in dismay. "Jesus, Valerie, what does it take to convince you of something?"

I glared at Russ. "Don't fight with me here," I thought. "Not now. Not in front of them." Russ just shook his head in disbelief.

"Proof," I answered slowly. "That's what it takes."

"Proof. It's proof that you want?" Russ responded. "Well how about this? How about writing my thoughts? How about St. Louis? How about the dreamscape? How about—"

"Stop it. I agree that there's a connection. It's just the word 'talking' that bothers me."

Joe spoke up. "I've read a lot of channeled work. Some that I believed. A lot that I didn't. This is real. I have no doubt. And the fact that it's the two of you together—that's really interesting. I'm so intrigued by your story."

I looked at Joe and did not speak. "Channeled," I thought. "Did you just say 'channeled'?" My mind was spinning. "If I can't accept talking, I certainly can't go with 'channeled.' Inspired, yes. Channeled, no." Once again, before I could elicit a tactful response, Russ was already speaking.

"Yeah, my wife channels angels, so I've read a fair amount of channeled work. But I've never read about something like this."

The waitress appeared and interrupted the conversation. She cleared the plates from in front of Joe and Ruth and then turned toward Russ and me. "Are you two finished?" she asked, raising her eyebrow. We looked down at our plates. They were barely touched.

"Yeah, I'm done," we said in unison.

"Was the food okay?" she asked. "Do you want it boxed?"

"It was great," I said. "Thank you. Just take it." I stared at the food as she stacked the plates on her hand. "Russ's stomach must feel like mine," I thought.

"Oh, look at the time," Ruth said. "I need to get back." She stood to leave. "Joe may be able to stay a little longer."

"One more cigarette," Joe responded, as Russ and I stood to embrace Ruth and thank her for setting up the meeting.

Russ hugged her first, and I stepped away from the table so that I could speak to her privately. I hugged her and thanked her with all of my heart. "You don't know how much this means to me," I whispered.

"Isn't he great?" she said, referring to Joe. "He's so encouraging. But only if he truly likes something. Only if he thinks it has merit."

My eyes welled with tears. Ruth smiled. She was a writer. She understood. "The writing is wonderful," she said. "Really." I hugged her once again before she turned and left the restaurant.

Russ stood to let me back in the booth while continuing his conversation with Joe. They were talking more generally about spiritual connections. "Look, this isn't about us," Russ said. "I mean the connection is there for anybody." He again settled back into his seat. "It really is a toll-free number."

"Toll-free number," Joe repeated. "I like that. I think you're right."

I only half-listened to their conversation. My thoughts were focused on all that had just transpired. I was amazed by the acceptance, not just of the writing but of the story. Joe and Ruth not only failed to reject our connection with Tahkamenon but seemed to embrace it, readily, joyfully.

Soon Joe got up to leave as well. Although we had just met, Russ and I hugged him too. We had shown him our souls, and he had been kind and gentle, taking the time to see the love behind the words. "I'd like to see more," he said.

"Certainly," I replied.

"Anything you want," Russ added.

"You have no idea how much this means to us," I said again, as I hugged Joe good-bye.

And in the most unsettling moment of the entire lunch, he looked me in the eye and responded, "I'm honored to be involved in this. I'll do whatever I can to help you get this message out."

"Thank you," I said, hugging him again and standing aside for Russ. "Is this a joke?" I thought. "Mr. author of four books and Pulitzer Prize judge, you're *honored* to be involved with us?"

Joe left, and Russ and I both took our places side by side in the booth. Once Joe was out of sight, we lost control. We hugged. We cried. We screamed. "Unbelievable," Russ shouted. The waitress looked over at us disapprovingly. Luckily, the lunch crowd had mostly dissipated, so we only made complete fools of ourselves in front of a very small crowd.

Russ turned and grabbed my shoulder. "One hundred percent publishable," he said. "Did you hear him? Did you?"

"Lyrical poetry with a message," I responded, resting my forehead on Russ's chest. We sat in the booth for a least another forty-five minutes, rehashing every detail of the conversation. "Publishable. Lyrical poetry. Honored to be involved." The waitress came by several times to fill our water glasses, bring coffee and finally notify us that she was leaving her shift.

"Can we borrow your pen?" Russ asked. The waitress pulled one from behind her ear. Russ passed it to me.

"Write something down," he said. "I don't ever want to forget this meeting." The waitress was fidgeting impatiently, so I quickly grabbed a restaurant napkin and wrote:

May 23, 1996
"lyrical poetry with a message"
—Joseph Dunn, author
Pulitzer Prize judge

I gave the pen back to the waitress. We sat a while longer, gloating and finishing our coffee. We finally left, but I pulled the car over into an apartment complex parking lot before returning to the office. We sat in the car, the sun streaming through the windows. We screamed some more, stamping our feet against the floor. I pounded the steering wheel. Russ shook the dashboard. We had to let out the craziness that consumed our bodies. Finally, I looked at Russ and smiled. "Unbelievable," I said, looking intently into his eyes.

"I knew that you would start to see things my way," he responded, smiling back and hugging me gently. "It really is unbelievable."

In the quiet of those moments before we returned to my office, I contemplated the impact of this luncheon. "We're going to do it," I thought. "We're really going to do it. We're going to write a book. We're going to spread this incredible message." As I bathed in the warmth of the implications, a small but persistent voice entered my consciousness. "I wonder what Joe meant by a marathon?" I thought as I pulled away from the curb.

Russ grabbed my arm before I could consider the question any further. "Did you get the napkin?" he asked in a panic.

"Yes. Of course," I responded.

"Where? Where is it? I want to see it."

"I have it. Leave me alone."

"I want it," Russ demanded.

"Too bad. You're not getting it," I answered.

"Why not? It's mine too," Russ pouted.

"Because I have it, and I'm keeping it."

"Fine. Keep it." Russ said. "But I'm taking notes at the next meeting."

"You do that," I answered as we arrived at my office.

"Just let me see it," he pleaded.

I pulled the napkin from my purse and let him hold it long enough to read the words. After a few moments, I quickly pulled it away.

"Somebody really should teach you to share," Russ said.

"I'll share my heart," I answered. "With you, I'll even share my soul. But the napkin?" I said, dangling it between us. "I'm keeping the napkin." I folded it and tucked it safely into the zippered compartment of my purse.

"I hope Tahkamenon knew what he was doing when he picked you," Russ said as we walked into the office.

"Only time will tell," I responded, picking up a stack of messages from the front desk and forgetting all about my marathon question. I should have considered it in more detail. Or maybe not. Maybe it was better that I didn't give Joe's warning any further thought.

Chapter Fourteen

The joy of that meeting with Joe and Ruth helped shake off any remnants of my depression. I was now ready to move forward. The world was opening up, the trees, the flowers, and the beauty in full bloom. Thankfully, I could see it all—the color, the texture, the hope. I started to write again. If Joe wanted more, I would gather what I had and add as much as I was able. I once again focused on the writing, accepting the connection, wanting only to give voice to the power of Tahkamenon's words:

My heart is open, my intentions true. It has been so long since we sat here together, yet I knew always that this again would be. I never cease to wonder at the power of distractions, of the maze of steps that seem so important until they are taken. But each step that leaves you empty was not meant to be, or at least not upon your true course. The necessity of the steps is not mine to question. I am here only to help you find your way.

We struggle so with form—you in your writing, I in my presentation. How best to find my way into your heart? How best to touch the recesses of your soul?

Over the next few days, I gathered what we had written. The passages consumed my living room floor, and I swam through the sea of words, bathing in wave after wave of significance.

What your mind sees as paradox, your heart knows as truth.

Paper was everywhere—yellow legal pads, pink notebook sheets, a bound composition book, Russ's faxes, his blue meeting notes, and various lines written on assorted scrap paper. I wanted to put them in order, but what order to use? By date? By ideas? By authorship?

Nothing seemed right. No matter how hard I tried to focus on the overall form, I kept getting caught in the power of each individual passage.

Hold my hand. I will lead you through the mysteries of your lifetime, through the questions of your world. I will take you to the waters, through the reflections of the surface, through the darkness and into the light.

"What words of encouragement," I thought, as I picked up more passages and continued to read.

I flow in the gentle ripples of the water, softly caressing your borders, quietly reminding you of my presence. You recognize me without effort, even in those moments when I do not touch the shore. You now know absolutely that I continue to exist, that eventually I will return.

You breathe me in the air. I sing to you in the whistling of the wind. I cool your body with the damp embrace of raindrops. But do not forget that you exist in each of these as well. Remember the unity. My perception may be different, my point of reference unique, yet I exist nowhere where you do not also.

The harmony of the vibrations of the elements of your world, a beautiful song, a recognizable rhythm. You change each moment that you touch, individually and collectively. You alter the vibrations with your presence, yet the basic rhythm remains, holding its integrity, true to its course.

Feel the cool embrace of the water, the rhythmic stirring of the ripples. You need not only embrace the underlying rhythm but also the distinct variations to completely understand.

Have you ever experienced such security? Have you ever known such peace? Whisper and hear the silent echo enfold you. Open your mouth to sing and watch the impact of each word upon the water. Experience the vibration of each expression of love upon the world.

I cried a lot as I went through the process, partly because of the frustration of trying to impose order but mostly as a result of the profound authenticity of the words. The words were mine, mine and Russ's, but they flowed from a higher level of inspiration. They touched me deeply. It was as if my soul had come alive within my body. I now visualized it as any of my other vital organs, deep within my center, attached directly to my heart.

You are divine, your soul protected. Remember in the struggle, you are spirit first, spirit forever, human for but the briefest flash of eternity.

I finally gave up on any real order and chose the pieces

haffazardly, placing them in a stack to type into my computer.

> Rejoice in those who have eclipsed the barriers. They are your beacons. They illuminate the possibilities. You recognize those of whom I speak in your family, your community, your history. Rare and magnificent, universal in their message, constant in their action.

> Do not focus on your humanness or the fact that the transformation is incomplete. It is the movement that matters now. It is the preparation. It is the shift in thought and alignment with your purpose. You can find your way back to the beauty of the spirit. You need only follow the guidance of your heart.

Typing helped. Somehow the conformity of the letters and the presence of the margins made the words themselves seem orderly and held the thoughts more securely within the structure of my mind.

> What is it that I ask of you? That you open your heart to the melody of the universe, that you see your reflection in the light of the stars, that you understand the profound power of the pyramids, that you embrace paradox, that you accept unity, that you love yourself so truly you cannot help but love each other.

I picked up a blue piece of paper with Russ's handwriting scrawled alongside notes from an earlier meeting. I read the words and thought again of the walls that we instill without intention, of the barriers that we perpetrate in the name of love.

> You teach your children. That does not permit the spirit to grow. For the spirit to grow, you must teach the unseen not the seen. The child newborn knows nothing but everything. Do you understand?

Does not the face of a child glow with a kiss from a parent? Who taught him so? Only with learning will the child tense up. What good for the child the learning? What good for the parent?

I treasured these moments immersed in these beautiful words. I valued the solace. I welcomed Tahkamenon's healing touch upon my soul.

I feel such love for you. Separated by worlds, in separate dimensions, and still a connection of such strength and importance that it is undeniable.

Is the connection distinct or integral? Are you human or spirit? Is God separate or innate?

The answer to each is both.

I eagerly read the words, my heart bolstered by their encouragement. I perceived a pattern—Tahkamenon spoke not of his power, which must be infinite, but of our own. Always the reminder that we were an active part of the message, that each person who heard the melody added to the beauty of the song. What security to understand that we could alter the vibrations but not diminish the integrity or rhythm of our souls.

Russ and I need only move forward, and he would be there to guide and protect us, to hold our hands, to embrace our hearts.

Hold my hand. Look into my heart. Allow yourself to know my soul. If you do so you will cease to question the motive of my words. You will see yourself reflected and illuminated with love.

I spent several weeks typing the writing into a readable format, and then we made plans to meet again with Joe and Ruth. This time we would include Brian and Mary Ellen as well. Having recovered from our initial fear of sharing our writing, we now looked forward to hearing Joe's input and to discussing the book in more detail.

Excited about the upcoming meeting and inspired by the power of the passages, I wrote still more to add to the mix.

This is a gift that grows with the giving, magnified and reinforced by each heart that it touches, each soul that finds a ray of light.

Focus on the writing, on hearing the message, on capturing the essence in your words. The rest is destined. You will find your way. I understand your need for definition, your desire to put this into final form, but recognize that it will never be final. This is a journey not a destination. And all are included, much more than you recognize, many more than you currently comprehend.

Trust in your ability to touch the hearts of others. Have you not always done this, with great compassion, with true love? It is nothing new that I ask of you.

You confuse yourself by adding difficulty onto such a simple task. Love each other. Speak the message so that others will hear. You are interpreters. I trust you with my essence because it is not mine. It is yours, and it is Russ's. It is the essence of each person who will hear.

I give you nothing. I give you yourself. I give you your own connection. You do not create the meaning. It exists separately, integral to your being just as you are integral to the meaning itself. You must break through linear thinking. Only on the physical plane do you process ideas in such a way.

Your spiritual self has the ability to see things more clearly. It sees the forest yet cannot fully comprehend the beauty of a single tree. The texture and color is yours alone to absorb. Each of you individually. You see the tree separately, from a different perspective within the physical plane. That is also a gift, a reason for choosing a lifetime in the physical world. Or maybe several lifetimes. Or maybe none at all.

Do you feel the beauty of your path? Are you enjoying the melody? Vibrating with the color and the light? I feel excited to be moving forward along the journey. You may think that I always move forward, but remember—I have chosen to walk this path with you.

I was invigorated by the words—"this is a gift that grows with the giving." "We are intended to share this message," I thought. "We're being asked to speak the truth."

I faxed the writing to Russ. He called a few minutes later.

"Hello, this is Valerie."

"Hello. Tahkamenon?"

"I'm sorry, Tahkamenon's not here right now. Can I take a message?"

"No, you're wrong," Russ answered. "Tahkamenon is here right now. And you can take a message. Beautifully, I might add."

"Okay, you're right. He is here. He was hiding—you know, somewhere here in my heart. Do you like it?"

"No. I love it."

"Really love it? Or just kind of love it?"

"Are you really insecure or just kind of insecure?"

"Both," I immediately responded.

"Stop it. It's wonderful." Russ paused for a moment before continuing. "Of course I always knew it."

"Always knew what? That my writing was wonderful?"

"No. Get over yourself. That's not what I meant. That we chose to be human," Russ answered. "I always knew that it was a choice."

"What a neat concept," I replied.

"Well it really is the only thing that makes sense. If we are eternally spirit, then becoming temporarily human must be a choice. I don't think that spirits have accidents."

"I don't know," I answered. "Tahkamenon did hook up with you."

"Oh, did I mention that the message is beautiful but the writing sucks?" Russ quickly replied.

"Okay, I surrender," I said, focusing again on the passage. "I love the way it starts—'this is a gift that grows with the giving.' How beautiful."

"Sounds like love," Russ said.

"It is love," I responded. "Oh, and what about this—'I give you nothing. I give you yourself?'" I continued to read the passage silently. Russ was quiet as well, either reading or thinking. I wasn't sure which.

"Do you feel the beauty of your path?" he asked, interrupting my thoughts.

"Sometimes," I answered. "Do you?"

"I guess sometimes too. But not enough. Not as much as I think is intended."

"Well, having all of these choices is terrific, but it can be a real pain in the ass. I mean, if there is a path that we are supposed to take, then why doesn't God just put us on it?"

"Yeah. Like why do we have all this responsibility?" Russ asked. "We're only human."

"Oh, but now you're wrong," I said. "We're also spirit. Always spirit. It's that invisible thing. It makes us forget."

"It's that invisible thing we need to remember," Russ replied, his voice soft and reverent.

"Sure is," I responded "Amazing how difficult that can

be. Hey," I said, switching gears, "do you know when you're coming?"

"Thursday, I think. Mary Ellen and Autumn can't wait to get to the beach. Have you confirmed yet with Joe and Ruth?"

"Yes. Dinner here on Saturday night. I'm really looking forward to it."

"It certainly should be interesting," Russ said.

"Yeah," I laughed. "Just wait until they reveal at dinner that they're talking to Tahkamenon too."

"We're all talking to Tahkamenon," Russ responded. "One way or another."

"Maybe," I said. "Some of us just seem to have more static on our lines than others." We were quiet for a moment. "Don't forget to call as soon as you know your schedule."

"I won't. Have you sent Joe the writing?"

"Not yet, but it's almost together."

"Well be sure to send him this new passage. It's beautiful."

"What? What was that? I can't hear you. You're breaking up. My line, it's full of static."

"Very funny," Russ responded. "Now you will get him the writing, right?"

"Of course I will. I'll send him everything. I can't believe this—two real authors and a Pulitzer Prize judge to boot." I was still amazed at how they had appeared in our lives at just the right moment. "How did we get so lucky?" I asked.

"Connections, darlin'. It's all about connections."

Chapter Fifteen

I sent Joe our passages and continued to write. The more I immersed myself in the message, the more I questioned the source of the words. I believed fully in Tahkamenon, yet I remained unsure as to what that belief actually meant. Did I believe that he was a distinct presence? Or a spirit? Or somehow a continuation of myself?

And what was the impact of the connection with Russ? Did I connect with Russ because of Tahkamenon or with Tahkamenon because of Russ?

I knew that I would not find the answers on the physical plane, but I was no longer afraid to ask the questions of my soul. So I turned to Tahkamenon and waited for his reply.

What courage it takes to face the question of your own divinity. What ability to suspend the feelings of guilt, the fear of arrogance, the imposition of the rules. Yet what simplicity. It is a logical leap—if you possess a spirit, then you are at least partially divine. And given that partial divinity, who would hazard to believe that it is the human part of your nature that holds the most significance? You easily label yourself human, but that is only what you see, not what you are.

So why the trepidation of accepting divinity? Because you are mortal? Well, only your cover, never your soul.

Interesting, but not really an answer. Still, I knew that I was moving. I was more aware of my spiritual dimensions. Strangely, I felt more aware of my humanity as well. Recognizing my dual existence as both human and spirit, I longed to integrate my spirit into my life.

All that you experience can be viewed from both humanity and divinity. Yet within your world of illusion, you have come to accept reality as that which you can see with your eyes and hold in your hands. You have discounted the significance of your spiritual perceptions, turning away from the power of your source. In doing so, you have created a void in your life that was never intended.

The physical component of your existence was given as a gift not a sentence—meant to illuminate the beauty of light broken down into color, to allow you to experience individual achievement and physical sensation. Yet in experiencing these you have come to discount the source. You derive meaning from things that lack eternal significance. There are few things that create meaning, but you have found it to be everywhere from your color to your age to your possessions.

You are divine. The mortal nature of your being is no match for the depth and immortality of your soul—a soul that you do not own so much as receive, a divinity made

stronger by a universal source and individual ramifica-
tions.

You have believed in your soul's existence throughout
the ages, throughout your plane. You recognize the
impact of those moments on the edge when you glimpse
the meaning from a distance. And yet you continue to
question your divinity as if it were foreign, as if it were
blasphemy.

You are divine, your soul protected. Feel the vibration,
the significance of these words. Repeat them in your
heart. Come to accept them as true. Past the fear, the
illusions of arrogance, find the faith to carry them always
by your side.

"We do need to question our beliefs," I thought, as I
wrote these words, both those of humanity and those of
divinity. The questions are simple—is this from my soul,
good for my soul, in line with my soul?—if only we could
find the courage to ask and the patience to listen.

I know that it is difficult, accepting that all your years
of searching, a humanity of searching, has brought you
back to yourself. Yet what other answer could there be?

The enduring nature of religion is a tribute to the truth
that it reflects. But it is shrouded in distortion. You
cannot accept religion because it is not pure truth. It is
reflection. It is distortion. It has been manipulated for
both good and bad, power and caring. And yet truth can
only come to you in love. It knows no other form. It
carries no other baggage.

So to learn acceptance you must practice on the truth.
Touch the eternal concepts. Religion holds many in its

bag of illusion. Do you feel the connection of one source? Now hold the moment. Feel the power of accepting the truth.

You are physically separate, mentally unique, yet which of these has meaning? Is not your soul the only true source of divinity? You know this from religion, but here is the twist. You are not less divine because you are human. You are not less connected because you are confused. You only fail to recognize your divinity because of your existence in the physical world.

It has been a difficult process in your world full of walls, in your world full of fear and deception. It all started with the notion that there must be a limit, that the beauty could not possibly be extended to each new soul. And then the struggle for power, the need to define those who were worthy to experience the blessings and those who were not.

You have been taught that divinity is separate and distinct from your human form. That the spirit is to be revered. That you do not have the ability to attain perfection. That many rules and men of great stature stand between you and a distinct divine presence that goes by many names and promises the answer to eternity.

What foolishness to believe that certain individuals could constrain the spirit. There is no gatekeeper other than yourself. There are no barriers that are not your own. So all of you are ministers, each the voice of the faith, each an example of the truth, each a beacon of the light.

Do you understand that you are not a passive part of this discussion? That the song is yours as well to sing? It is my purpose to fan the flames of your warmth so you may ignite others by your presence and your love.

I could not think of my soul without contemplating religion. The two intertwined in the mind. I had learned the connection as a child, but my feelings were mixed. Religion had served both to unite and divide us. So what was the place of religion? Was it an answer? Or merely a step?

Your religions grant too much power to the physical plane. They would have you believe that you can overcome the spirit with your actions, fall from the light as if there truly existed anywhere else to go. But your actions cannot remove your divinity; your thoughts cannot conquer your soul. You are not caught between the worlds of heaven and hell but have chosen to exist as both human and spirit. A choice you may question but will come with time to understand.

Humanity has proven its ability to move as a wave, to evolve in the physical sense, to reach greater and greater intellectual heights. You have evolved spiritually as well, no longer throwing virgins into volcanoes to pacify the gods. And yet this rule, this practice, was once held sacred. It was created by man and infused with the significance of relevance to the spirit. And those who practiced these sacrifices, both those who threw and those who were thrown, had to medicate their minds to suppress the doubt that lurked beneath the surface.

Who could doubt their belief when they chose to hurl the most beautiful and precious among them into a fiery grave? But were it not for the doubt, there would have been no need for the sacrifice. Do you understand the relationship? The sacrifices created more fear, fostered more doubt, and generated the need for greater and greater displays of their faith.

Are your religions today so different, condemning those who do not comply to the fiery depths of hell? If your God is everything, what then is the devil? If you understand God as the integration of your souls, from what is the devil composed? If heaven exists within you, if you are by your very nature divine, where then are you to find the misery of hell?

Have you thought that you've created this, with your fear and your hatred, that it is no more real than your illusions of evil? It is difficult I know, but for now it is enough to ask the questions and let them lie within your being. Answers are not always helpful. The truth can be quite unsettling until you have learned to accept.

In contrast to my earlier fear, I relaxed into this writing, trusting that the words were not harmful, knowing that they flowed from my soul. The writing no longer scared me. Even the initial passage on religion now seemed self-evident, not frightening. As I wrote these words, I saw them only for their beauty. I accepted their authenticity. I held them for their light.

Now you must move past the lessons that in many ways have defined your existence on the physical plane, learning to look both upward and inward. You have been taught of the existence of the spirit, of the power of truth, of the search for the light. You have been given many obstacles, none strong enough to extinguish the faith. But the lights have been dim, the melody distant for so long now that you have come to think of your soul as foreign. Yet it is the obstacles that you live with, those that you continue to create, that are foreign to the spirit.

It all seems so simple when you accept the connection and act solely from the impetus of love. You will find your path. It will lead you home. You will lead others even as you follow the footsteps of those who have tread the path before. It is a course that more and more will travel, a road that will become all the clearer with the use.

The answer to the question of religion lies not in the rules of exclusion, not in the sacrifice, but in the beauty and authenticity of the message. It is not the message that is debated; it is the distractions. It is the items given relevance by man that bear no relationship to the spirit.

Focused on the controversy, on the vehicle, you have turned away from the issues of true importance. Love thy neighbor. Love thyself. Believe in the meaning of your existence. Understand the insignificance of your constraints. Accept the connection. Cease valuing the distinctions. Test each movement close to your heart.

Before I finished the passage, I was driven to add:

Do not be deceived by the simplicity of these words. They break the barriers of many lifetimes and vibrate with an eternity of light.

I did not send these passages to Russ but saved them instead to share in person. On the day that we were to meet with Ruth and Joe, Russ and I sat and read over the writing together. "Do you remember what you wrote a few months ago?" I asked as soon as Russ looked up from the papers.

"Could you give me a hint?" he answered.

"It was about the message. It was perfect. 'This is the voice of peace you have heard forever.'"

"I remember," Russ said. "It is perfect."

"I've thought a lot about it. The peace part." I wanted

to continue but the words escaped me. Russ waited. I finally spoke. "I've always believed that this was the voice of peace, and yet the words have been so difficult. They've been controversial. They've addressed issues that I thought best left alone. But when I read this, I felt differently. The writing has not been controversial, not from a spiritual perspective, not if we view the words with love."

I paused again, and Russ remained silent so I continued on with my thoughts. "The writing questions our beliefs but never our heart; it judges our intentions but never our souls." My voice grew louder, energized by the power of the words. "Of course we are divine. We *are* both human and spirit—almost everyone believes that. We accept our humanity. Why not our divinity?"

"Because of the impact," Russ answered. "If we believed, it would change everything."

"Why?" I asked in frustration. "Why is it so difficult? Haven't we always acknowledged our souls?"

"Well, we usually *say* that we have one," Russ answered. "But I don't think that we consider the implications. We may acknowledge our souls but not the logical conclusion. And this," he continued, pointing to the pages in front of him, "this is even more than acknowledgment. It's acceptance. If we truly embraced our souls, it would change our perspective, our beliefs, our expectations. Hey, at least there's no hell," Russ added. "That's quite a relief."

"Maybe," I said. "For some people at least. And I think that it's time for a change. It feels like everything is changing already. Not just with us or because of this connection, but people in general seem more open, more ready." We both silently read the passages again. "I like what Tahkamenon is saying," I said. "That we do not have to forsake our humanity in order to appreciate our souls. That makes so much sense. Otherwise there is no need to be human."

"How did we ever come to believe that our humanity was stronger than our spirit?" Russ asked. "I mean, it's crazy. On one side we have love, truth, eternity, perfection. On the other we have fear, deception, mortality." We were both quiet and then Russ continued, "Suddenly it seems so straightforward. Do you think it's any more complicated than that?"

"Only when we make it so," I answered, flipping again through the passages. I enjoyed talking with Russ about the writing. The more we wrote and the more we talked, the deeper I fell into my consciousness. And no matter the depth of the connection, I did not forsake being human. Not only was it impossible, it did not even seem desirable. I appreciated my humanity, my ability to enjoy the distinction of our world.

I gathered the papers together to clear the table and get ready for dinner. As I did so, I quickly reread the final lines.

Do not be deceived by the simplicity of these words. They break the barriers of many lifetimes and vibrate with an eternity of light.

"Thanks for the warning, Tahkamenon," I thought, smiling at his divine guidance. "Just when we get to the peaceful part of the message, you have to go and remind us of the difficulty that lays ahead."

"What are you thinking about so intently?" Russ asked.

"Oh nothing really," I answered. "Just how fortunate we are to be a part of this incredible journey."

Chapter Sixteen

We were lucky, yes, but we were also confused. Very, very confused. The message was clearer, but the mechanics of forming the concepts into a book perplexed us. We hoped that the meeting with Joe would answer our questions. Unfortunately, he showed up with quite a few questions of his own.

The evening started well. While the children played together, Joe, Ruth, Russ, Mary Ellen, Brian, and I all talked about the book. We talked about the connection. We talked about Tahkamenon. We talked a great deal about our souls.

Joe again warned of the difficulty of writing a book. He asked Mary Ellen and Brian if they were willing to support this endeavor. Were they comfortable with the relationship? Were they willing to share us with the message?

They were wonderful, both of them. Each agreed, with conviction. We could not have asked for more support. They thought that the connection should be fostered.

They supported working toward a book. Mary Ellen remarked that reaching even one person was an admirable cause. That was nice. It eased the pressure. They eased our hearts.

Ruth had read more of the Tahkamenon writing and praised its startling simplicity. She compared and contrasted the concepts to other books that I had never read. Russ had, though, he and Mary Ellen. They, along with Joe and Ruth, were active participants in the growing spiritual movement. Brian and I listened to the conversation as outsiders, appreciating the dialogue but rarely taking part.

Then Joe took Russ and me inside to discuss more concretely the writing we had sent. Here the evening turned for the worse. While Joe praised the depth and clarity of the individual passages, he questioned the format in detail. "How are we going to know who wrote what?" he asked as we sat down at the table. "Which is your writing and which is Tahkamenon's?"

Russ and I looked at each other in silence. It was *our* writing—all of ours. What did he mean?

When we did not respond, Joe grew more abrupt. "What about this one?" he asked, holding up a passage for both of us to see.

"Well . . . I . . . I actually wrote that one," I answered, "but of course it's Tahkamenon's as well."

"Now, is it yours, or is it Tahkamenon's?" Joe asked. I turned to Russ for support.

He looked as confused by these simple questions as I. "Well, I don't think that Tahkamenon can write," Russ answered. "I mean not physically."

"I know that he can't write physically," Joe said, his voice louder, more forceful. "But how are you going to separate the writing for the reader? How will they know when you're talking, when Val's talking—"

"Or the Big T?" Russ interrupted.

"Yes," Joe replied. "Or the Big T. Do you see what I mean? This is all mixed together."

"But we don't think of it separately," I said.

"Well, unless you want the readers to be confused, you're going to have to," Joe responded, looking at me intently. I silently returned his gaze.

"Look," Russ said, trying to break the tension, "this isn't a problem. I'm sure that we can go through and figure out what Valerie wrote and what I wrote if you like." I started to object but stopped in response to Russ's glare. "So what else?" he continued. "Is there anything else that we need to do?"

"Do you have it all dated?" Joe asked. "The original writing, I mean."

"Sure," I answered, trying to reestablish a rapport. "Most of it is anyway."

"Well, that's good. It would be interesting to see the order in which you received it." Joe looked at me directly. "Now, when you wrote it or typed it in, did you change the words at all or are these exactly as he said them?"

My face flushed, and I bit down to hold my tongue. "I'm not taking dictation here," I screamed in my head, but the generosity of Joe's interest kept me from voicing my response.

Russ spoke as I gathered my thoughts. "Joe, I don't know that these are word for word. I'm not even sure—" Russ hesitated, looking down at the writing.

When he failed to continue, I picked up on his line of thought. "We're not trying to be difficult," I said softly. "We really appreciate what you're doing. Your questions are logical." I paused myself, searching for words. "And we certainly don't want the readers to be confused."

"But," Russ interjected, "we've never thought about the

writing so discretely. It's just ours, all of ours. When Valerie writes Tahkamenon, it sounds one way. When I write him, it sounds another. But the message is the same. It always—"

"So you do change his words," Joe interrupted, and we fell into an uneasy silence. We sat for a few moments, staring at the papers on the table. "What about the two of you?" Joe eventually asked. "You're going to need to write about yourselves, about how you met and all this started."

"You really think so?" I asked, surprised.

"Well it needs some context," Joe answered. "And your story is certainly compelling."

Russ shifted in his seat. I sensed his discomfort as I dealt with my own. For the next several minutes, we mostly agreed with everything Joe said, taking in his suggestions, not questioning his assumptions or trying to explain our relationship any further. We understood that Joe was an editor. He was doing exactly what he needed to do. He asked the right questions. We only responded with such frustration because we couldn't give him a reasonable reply.

At our first opportunity, we joined the others and tried to soothe the tension before Joe and Ruth left. "Thanks for everything," I said as they were leaving.

"Yeah," Russ added. "We know what you're saying. We'll go back through the writing and try to sort it all out."

We all hugged and said good night. As soon as Joe and Ruth pulled away, I turned to Russ. "I feel like I was just hit by a train."

"Don't worry," Russ said. "We can do this. We just need to put it in some kind of order, that's all."

I glared at Russ. "I did try to put it in order," I hissed. "For several weeks, in fact. But if you think *you* know who's talking when and what words belong to whom, then go ahead, take your best shot."

"Calm down, Valerie. He was only trying to help."

"I know that he was trying to help," I said as we sat down together on the front porch. "That's not why I'm angry. I'm angry because they are pretty goddamn simple questions, and we don't have any answers. We don't even know who's talking. How the hell are we ever going to write a book?"

"We *are* going to write a book," Russ replied, "because how else are we going to spread the message?"

I watched Brian and Mary Ellen through the screen door. They were cleaning up from dinner and negotiating treats with the children. "Maybe Mary Ellen's right. Maybe we're trying to do too much. Maybe we should just go around and share these ideas with one person at a time."

"Well," Russ said with a sigh, "that's going to make it awfully damn hard to 'touch the hearts of millions.' But if that's how you want to do it, hey, I'm there for you."

I laughed and looked at my watch. "We don't have a whole hell of a lot of time here," I said, putting my hand on Russ's leg. "We probably had better get started."

Russ laughed as well and squeezed his arm around my shoulders. "Don't worry," he repeated. "We're going to figure this out."

"Promise?" I asked.

"Promise," he answered.

I looked into his eyes, trying to detect any trace of doubt. But they were clear and focused. So one more time along an often difficult journey I decided to trust that somehow we would find our way. A few moments later we rounded up the kids, exchanged hugs and ended one of the most difficult evenings of our lives.

As painful as that night had been, it was nothing compared with the struggle that quickly ensued. Russ and I agreed that we were supposed to write a book. We believed it. But that one answer spawned a multitude of questions. Why was this happening to *us*? There were plenty of professional writers and spiritual leaders who would know what to do. Why choose us when we didn't have a clue?

"Come on, Tahkamenon," I said in frustration. "Don't you care about credentials? Don't you care about the message? Don't you care about our pain?"

Tahkamenon's response was brief and direct.

For all that you have, you have little more than your soul. For all that you lack, you lack for nothing of importance.

So we struggled with the words, with each other, with ourselves. We worked to forge the writing into a book, trying to connect the individual parts of the message. We fought desperately to superimpose a physical form.

Each phrase and each sentence burst with significance, tying themselves to words that came before and those that came after with an abiding connection and an undeniable support. But the structure was not of our world. We tried to reduce the connection to paper, fearing that we were not up to the task. These passages were not linear. They related and interrelated in our hearts, our souls, our connection with each other and our connection with our world.

How then to find order? How to integrate these beautiful words into a book and, even more importantly, into our lives?

This pain that you experience, much like your confusion, is the result not of the truth but of your inability to synthesize the truth with the reality you have created and come to believe through the years.

Do you recognize impatience as not allowing acceptance to occur? You are constantly moving, sometimes farther, sometimes closer, circling at times, but rarely quiet. You find it hard to accept while in motion, always thinking that the answer, your salvation, remains around the next turn.

It is amusing to me even as I wish to grab hold of your body and whisper to your soul—hold your motion for a moment. The truth is eternal. Your soul is divine. The answers are within you if only you will allow yourself enough peace to hear the melody, to flow within the rhythm, to find comfort in the words.

Why do you think that you are always in motion? What drives you to search for meaning as if it lay hidden, waiting only to be found? Why do you struggle so with the truth?

You will never experience peace as a people until you experience peace within yourself. Peace, like truth, exists, a creation of the spirit not of man. It cannot be removed by your foolishness; you can only be removed from its gentle caress.

As always, you remain part of the spirit, integral to the energy, significant in your soul. It may appear otherwise in your physical plane where you are lost in the sea of faces, different in color, texture, and age—more distraction but not even the hint of meaning. Are you beginning to understand?

The message is simple. It applies without fail. It works in each moment, in each lifetime, in each soul. I try to explain the power within the limits of your language, within the confines of your linear mind. And still I know that you are capable of transcending these barriers, of far greater comprehension, if you will only come to believe in yourself.

That is the answer. Not believing in me. Not believing in words or in thoughts or in actions. But in yourself. It is all there, carefully presented within a context you will come to understand.

I stopped, read the passage, and then added to the end:

I express these thoughts not to enlighten but to remind.

"Maybe you should remind us less and enlighten us more," I thought. "Because this way doesn't seem to be working very well."

In response to my exasperation, Tahkamenon grew more direct. I had asked so many questions. He now chose to ask some of his own.

What is it that you have to lose by accepting this message and following your path? Are you afraid of your own intentions? Do you fear the contents of your heart? And while you run from yourself, you continue to allow the physical world to guide your actions. You continue to experience both emptiness and pain, the comfort of the known stronger than the promise of the truth. And yet you know that not to be.

Nothing in your world is stronger than the truth that I long for you to experience. But you must understand that I feel no sadness in this moment. It is a journey not a destination. I am happy in knowing the beauty of the movement even when it appears that the way is long and that you are weary.

I have chosen to walk with you not just for your benefit but for my own.

I finished the passage and called Russ. "Do you know what he said?" I shrieked. "What he accused me of?"

"Who said?" Russ asked. "What are you talking about? Are you all right?"

"No, I'm not all right. And I'm talking about Tahkamenon. That's who."

"Uh oh," Russ said, laughing. "I knew that it was just a matter of time before he really pissed you off."

"Go to hell."

"There is no hell," Russ responded. "Don't you read any of this stuff?"

"I hate you. Of course I read it, that's why I'm so angry. Listen to this," I said, and I read Russ the passage. "Do I fear the contents of my heart?" I asked as I finished reading. "The contents of my heart? What type of stupid asinine question is that?"

"It doesn't sound like a stupid question. I think—"

"Look I don't really care what you think. It is a stupid question. What do I fear? Does he want to know what I fear? I fear a whole hell of a lot of things. I fear the government. I fear the violence that surrounds me. I fear for my children. I fear that I can't write this book. I fear—"

"Valerie, calm down."

"But what I don't fear is my heart. What the hell kind of question is that?"

"Obviously, a very sensitive one."

"Don't even take that tone with me. It's not sensitive. It's stupid. I would have expected more from a spirit."

"Sounds like he expects more from you."

"Good-bye, Russ."

"Good-bye, Pumpkin."

Russ and I had several discussions, arguments actually, as we tried to make our way through the book. And the more we asked for help with the layout, the more we wrote about choices and paths. Was there a relationship? Were we missing the point? If Tahkamenon wanted us to spread this message, why was he making it so difficult to figure out how?

Your journey is destined, the momentum preordained, but the speed of your movement is a choice that you make. You will go individually and together, some running ahead, others dragging behind; but the movement in your collective consciousness will be dramatic and distinct. Each new being born into existence on the physical plane will start the journey ahead of those who tread the path before. So it is within their purpose, within their destiny, to move you even further along the road.

At first it may be slow, one barrier at a time. You have taught your feet to walk false paths. The truth will feel different. You tend to slow at that which is not familiar. Yet this path that you have chosen is more familiar than you think, familiar to your heart, recognizable by your soul.

I am humored by the struggle because I know that you will find your way. That much is destined. Eventually you each will return home. Eventually you will come to accept yourself.

Do not be discouraged even when the way is long, filled with more barriers than you care to acknowledge. Having chosen to walk this path, you must allow yourself to cherish the beauty of the moment, to experience fully the exhilaration of the movement.

At times you may choose to step off of the path. For now the journey may seem lonely, isolated from the perceptions and understanding of those you love and trust. But you cannot give up the way easily once you have felt the stirrings in your heart, once you have experienced the warming of your soul. You will step back onto your path when you are ready, reassured that you have been chosen as a leader just as surely as you have chosen to accept your role.

Why did Tahkamenon keep talking about choices when all that we wanted was the order of the words and the clearest relationship between the thoughts? How did the parts fit together? What was the message? How could we present a comprehensive whole?

You are both a piece of the puzzle and the universal truth the puzzle strives to represent. A single note that vibrates with the entire melody. Simultaneously an instrument and a symphony. This is the concept that defies your linear thinking. You are each a part, yet the whole exists within you, within each of you, each piece shining with the truth.

It appears a reversal on the physical plane, the whole within a part, but not in the spiritual. Understand that each piece holds the answer. Each piece is the answer. The placement merely serves your need to see. The puzzle need not be complete for you to understand and accept. Yet in your acceptance, the picture will be clear.

Paradox exists only in your world, a by-product of linear thinking. Acceptance of the power of the third dimension holds the key to all that is spiritual, to all that is universal. When you abandon linear logic, truth appears clearly within your heart, not to be seen but to be understood.

You have the advantage of being both human and spirit, both limited and limitless. If only you would come to accept this, your understanding would be complete.

This is the promise of the physical world.

"Nice promise," I snapped, "but how about some real guidance? Why don't you just show us which path we are supposed to choose?"

> Remember always that each step holds the answer. Each piece of the puzzle is representative of the whole. You will recognize your course when you become accustomed to experiencing the truth. Imagine that each step holds fulfillment in and of itself.

> Do you understand the difference this will make in the emptiness of your life? It means that you alone have the ability to alter your course. You have been programmed to focus on the destination, so you accept the emptiness and isolation of the path and justify the pain as a means to an end. Now you must focus on each step, individually and in progression, finding meaning in the movement, finding love in each moment of your travel.

> Why are you so afraid to accept the truth? Is not the promise of fulfillment preferable to the loneliness that you now experience? You are lonely not for lack of contact with each other, but for lack of contact with the truth. You are empty because you do not allow each moment to vibrate with love. And now I offer you a way that vibrates always in the light and ask that you allow its warmth to penetrate your soul.

Russ and I read the words in frustration but could not help but draw from their encouragement. So we crept forward in confusion, struggling with the layout, the order, the context. But not with the content. That never slowed us. We never questioned the truthfulness of the words that filled our hearts and poured from our souls.

Through this moment, you enter eternity. The spirit exists only in the present, not in the past, not in the future. This moment alone vibrates with potential. And the choices that you make today alter your course, define your path.

The stirrings of this moment will ripple through your life, creating large waves, rolling out toward distant shores. You are one with the spirit. We are one with each other.

I come to lead you home, not by force but by the weight of your own desire. I have come to remind you of your ability to define your course. So it is now upon you to embrace the spirit, to step upon your path, to find the courage to follow your heart.

It is within your ability. It is within your destiny.

Have faith.

And we did. So the words continued. Words more of guidance than of direction. Tahkamenon refused to give us the order, only the indication that each piece, each passage, held the answer within. So I focused less on the placement and more on the movement, trying to step without fearing the repercussions. Still I tripped over the physical alignment as I concentrated on the content. I continued to question the need for this form, for a book to contain a message, for a body to contain a soul.

Tahkamenon quickly reminded me of the delusion of my thoughts.

Ah, but that is the illusion you have come to believe. Your soul is not contained within your body; your body exists always within the power of the spirit. The spirit is within you and without, comforting your center, guiding your path.

I searched for the courage to trust in my soul, to stop playing the victim, to embrace my heart. Inspired by Tahkamenon, I began to view my humanity not as a shield but as a tool, a method of definition, a symbol of faith.

It is your fear, not your body, that constrains your soul. Only that which is unseen has the power to hold you back. And even that, even your fear, even your doubt, has the power to restrain you only so long as you allow it. You can never renounce your spirit; but each moment is a unique opportunity to forsake your fear, to follow your heart, to fill your life with love.

Understand that the power of the spirit surrounds you, permeating your being, saturating your existence. It is a wonder that for so long you have ignored that which is everywhere, and yet it is precisely those things that are with you without fail that you often refuse to see. You focus on the search and forget what you are looking for, so easily distracted, so obviously worn from the effort.

Well, that much was right. I was certainly "worn from the effort." But I was also sustained by the beauty of the message. The words touched me. They changed me. "Each moment is a unique opportunity to forsake your fear, to follow your heart, to fill your life with love." What a statement of freedom. The previous steps did not matter. The present would not be constrained by the past. Each moment remained mine for the choosing, each step mine for the taking.

A game plan formed in the recesses of my mind. I felt more than knew it—a vague recognition of the patchwork of choices that made up my life. I heard the faintest of melodies, the most familiar of sounds. It was only much later, much deeper, that I could look back and hear the sound for what it was.

It was my soul in the distance, whispering softly to my heart.

Chapter Seventeen

"You're never going to believe the dream I had last night," I said as soon as Russ answered the phone.

"Who is this?" he asked. "Do I know you?"

"Shut up. You have to hear this."

"Shut up. Shut up? Is that what this relationship has come to?"

"Russ! Come on. It really frightened me. I'm still scared."

"Okay. Okay," Russ said, as he covered the receiver with his hand. "Donna, close my door, will you? Okay. I'm ready." His voice cleared. "Now, it wasn't sexual was it?"

"No, not really, not unless spiders and bears happen to turn you on. Now stop kidding around. I'm really upset."

"I'm sorry. Spiders and bears, huh? What happened?"

"Well, it all started like I was going to play baseball."

"Can you even play baseball?"

"Very well, thank you. Now listen."

"I am listening. You're playing baseball with spiders and bears—"

"No! Stop interrupting. I'm going to play baseball with everyone from my office."

"You mean like Cindy and Terry and Andrea?"

"Yes. Only when I get—"

"Can they play baseball?"

"Good-bye, Russ."

"What do you mean 'good-bye'? I thought that you were going to tell me your dream."

"I hate you."

"Does that mean you *are* going to tell me the dream or you're not going to tell me the dream?" I did not respond. "Val, Val, are you there?"

"Yes," I answered.

"Hey," Russ said, his voice gentle. "I'm sorry. I'll quit playing. This dream really did get to you, didn't it?"

"That's what I'm trying to tell you."

"Okay. I'm listening. I promise."

"Look, I go to play baseball, only when I get there, it's not a regular field. It's a stadium, with bleachers and microphones and people all over. It's almost like a carnival—vendors with popcorn, balloons, and cotton candy. Men are lining the field with white chalk."

"Wow. Sounds like your playing in the big leagues."

"Yeah. That's what it looks like. I'm looking around, amazed because I think I'm just going to play a game with the people from work. And then I see the bear."

"The bear," Russ repeated. "Now was he selling anything?"

"No. Stop it. He wasn't selling anything. He was in a cage near the pitcher's mound. He was so big. He filled the entire cage. I figured that he must be some form of entertainment. The bleachers filled with spectators. Here it gets fuzzy, but I went behind the bleachers and warmed up and then started back out on the field. The vendors were gone, but the bear was still there. Only now he was out of his cage. He didn't move and kept looking from one place to the next as if searching for an escape. Someone pulled me aside, I can't remember who, and told me that the purpose of the game was to throw balls at the bear and to try to get him to run around in different directions."

"I would have checked out right about there," Russ interjected.

"Yeah, well, me too. Except just as I understood the rules, I was out on the field, and the crowd rose to its feet, thundering with applause. I wanted to run, but I couldn't. I couldn't let everyone down. Besides, I didn't want anyone to think that I was a chicken."

"You mean, as opposed to a lunatic?"

"Yeah. Pretty much. So I walked up to home plate with a ball in my hand. The bear was huge and agitated by the noise. He looked at me briefly. I saw fear in his eyes. That frightened me even more. The noise grew deafening. I pulled back my arm and threw the ball as hard as I could."

"Oh my God," Russ said. "What happened?"

"I hit him. Right in the chest. For a moment, he didn't even move. Then he shook his head slowly, rolled down on all fours and came toward me."

"What did you do?"

"I ran. What do you think I did? I ran as fast as I could, and he was running behind me. And then I saw Terry and Cindy in the bleachers. They started to throw things from the stands, soda cans and such. Everyone else threw things as well. They distracted the bear, and I got away."

"That's great, but where does the spider come in?"

"I'm getting there," I replied. "Don't rush me."

"Excuse me, but I can't take the suspense."

"Imagine how I felt. I was scared to death. Anyway, I ran along the bleachers and out an opening into the parking lot. Brian was waiting there in a car with the kids in the back seat and the passenger door open. So I jumped in the seat, pulled the door closed, and Brian sped off. It took me a moment to catch my breath. I was so relieved to have escaped the bear. And then I saw the spider."

"The spider," Russ said dramatically. "I knew we would get to the spider."

"Well, he was there all right, perched on top of the seat between me and Brian. He was big like a tarantula, only longer and thinner. And he was smooth, not furry. No one else seemed to notice him."

"Just like your chanting angel," Russ said.

"Yeah, I guess. I hadn't thought of that. Anyway, I didn't want to scare the children, so I just watched the spider out of the corner of my eye. He made me really nervous."

"I'll bet."

"We drove for a while. I didn't know where we were going. I kept one eye on the road and one on the spider. Finally, I turned to look fully at Brian just as he slammed on the brakes. The spider leapt from the back of the seat toward my lap. It sailed through the air and seemed to pass through some invisible shield. As it did, its skin just melted away."

"Gross."

"By the time it landed on the seat beside me, it was a grayish white skeleton."

"Then what happened?"

"I woke up."

"Well, here's a word of advice. Next time wake up as soon as you see the bear on the field."

"Oh, thank you, Russ. You're always so helpful." We sat for a moment in silence, contemplating the bizarre nature of my dream.

"Wow, that must have been pretty frightening," Russ said after a few moments.

"Yeah. I'm still scared. And I can't really explain it, but I couldn't turn back. I just had to face that bear once I was out on the field."

"So, do you think the bear was the Department of Labor?" Russ asked, referring to my fight with the government.

"I don't know," I answered, the images vivid in my mind. "Big, scary, intimidating—could be. But the spider bothers me more."

"Yeah, that part is pretty creepy." Again we were silent. "It's skin just melted away?" Russ finally asked.

"Just like that. I don't know if he was dead or just a skeleton."

"What the hell does that mean? Do you know any live skeletons?"

"I don't know. Leave me alone," I answered, confused by my own statement. "Don't you think I've been through enough for one day?"

"I'll say. I don't know if I'd ever go to sleep again."

"Believe me, I haven't quite settled that question myself."

We moved on to business and left the dream to fester in my memory. I felt anxious and afraid. What was its message? I could accept that the bear represented the government, large and clumsy, moving slowly until it turned on its prey with incredible speed and accuracy. But what about the spider? I felt that the spider was more intimate, not representative of the establishment, but something closer, something scarier, something less easily distracted.

And I wasn't only upset about the dream. The whole situation with the government was playing on my mind. I felt paranoid and cynical. Nothing seemed as simple as before. I questioned everyone's motives. I questioned our beliefs as a country. I questioned my place in the whole.

I decided to ask Tahkamenon, to focus on my fear and see if he would provide any insight. So late that night, worn from the day and the aftermath of the dream, I pulled out my notebook and wrote:

Why have I forsaken you? Do not allow yourself such folly. No one can forsake you but yourself. I remain always, constant in my love, watching as you resist the vibrations and shelter yourself from the healing powers of the light.

Have you not learned the destructiveness of walls? And yet you continue to build, brick after brick, surprised at the darkness and the absence of heat.

How can I teach you to live without fear? The answer is faith. Not in me but in yourself, in your being, in the spirit of which we share.

The walls of others also impede your movement. You must free them even as you free yourself. Their walls are their own to transcend, yet you can provide security, an example of truth, a personification of joy.

You are so filled with beauty, with perfection, with light; yet you allow yourself to experience only the damp emptiness of the passageways. Feel my words as many wings upon your soul. Imagine only beauty. See the water and the children. Sway with the vibration of the trees and the fish. Walls cannot withstand the intensity of the vibrations. They will wither away in the heat of the light. But only if you allow this. Only if you come to fully embrace the truth.

What are your options? Both sorrow and pain. Yet you continue to choose the darkness, continue to forsake the light. Open your heart. Follow the vibrations of your soul. Draw others to the warmth of the truth.

It is as if you are sleeping, tormented at night by some terrible dream. Each time that I nudge you, you awaken briefly and smile at the recognition of your surroundings. And you understand that the horror is not real, even though only moments before it consumed your senses and fed upon your fear.

You relax once more into the dream and again experience the terror as if you had no knowledge of its lack of integrity, no proof of its lack of existence. You do this continually, night after night, day after day. I beg you to waken, to pull fully from your slumber, defying the force of the terror, overcoming the impact of the pain.

I stopped writing for a moment, amazed that Tahkamenon was responding to my concern over the dream so directly. After reading the words, I continued to write.

Allow the warmth of the light to shine from your eyes and sparkle in your smile. Allow your touch to heal the open wounds of those that surround you. You must embrace them, even those who do not yet see. Especially those who do not yet see. Remember their walls. These barriers too must be transcended.

Believe in your ability to do this. For when you reach through the brick to touch the heart of another, he will come to understand that his walls are not invincible, that the path to the light is within his own reach.

Of course he too may lapse into a fitful sleep and then you may nudge him as I do you. Eventually, he will come to accept the beauty of waking, of tearing down the walls and standing freely in the light. Unencumbered by his fear and his jealousies, he will be able at last to reach through the barriers of another, continuing this pattern until the collective movement is freer than you now have the ability to understand.

But it starts here in this moment, with you, with one foot upon the journey, with one heart defying the constraints of your fear. Choose love. Test the path. Come to recognize the vibration of the light as you recognize the voice of a friend.

You must learn to suspend your reactions, the ones you have been taught throughout the ages of humanity, the ones that fail the invariable test of your soul. You must suspend these willfully and allow yourself the ability to experience the truth. And soon you will waste no effort on the suspension. That which is false will fall from your being. Then you will come to see me clearly, without guidance, without fear.

Why have I forsaken you? I can never forsake you. You will come to accept the impossibility of this and only then will your fear truly subside.

I read the words to Russ the next morning. He was quiet at first, allowing them to filter through his mind. "Well, there you go," he said, breaking the silence at last. "You want to talk to him about your dream, and he talks about a dream. That Tahkamenon. He's one hell of a spirit, don't you think?"

"Yeah, he's just terrific. Only I wish he wouldn't turn everything back to my own responsibility. I'm already overwhelmed as it is."

"He's not asking much," Russ responded. "Just overcome your own fears and help everyone else overcome theirs. Hell, I've seen you do more than that before breakfast."

"Thanks for the encouragement. But remember, you signed up for this duty as well."

"Oh well, now that's different. See Tahkamenon and I have this deal—"

"No. There is no deal. Not without me." I scanned the handwritten pages again as I spoke. "Boy, he pisses me off. 'Feel my words as many wings upon your soul.' Pretty words, Tahkamenon. Why didn't you fly me the hell out of that stadium?"

"It seems to me that he did," Russ responded.

"Oh sure. And right into a car with some monster spider skeleton."

"Maybe there are some things that he can't fly you away from."

I could feel the blood rushing to my face. "Maybe you can just go—"

"Read it to me again," Russ interjected.

"What again?" I asked, irritated at his tone.

"The passage. Read it to me."

"I'll type it tonight and fax it."

"Just read it for God sakes." Russ sounded irritated himself.

I read him the passage. I was edgy at first, but the beauty of the words calmed my heart and soothed my soul.

"There. Stop there," Russ exclaimed. "Read that part again."

"What part?"

"It all starts here," Russ answered. "Read that part."

"Why do I put up with you?"

"Because you can't help yourself. Now read. Please."

"Okay but only because you said 'please.'" I smiled and

returned to the start of the paragraph. 'But it starts here in this moment, with you, with one foot upon the journey, with one heart defying the constraints of your fear. Choose love. Test the path. Come to recognize the vibration of the light as you recognize the voice of a friend.'"

"Damn, that's beautiful," Russ whispered.

"Do you want me to finish?" I asked.

"Yeah. Now I'm ready."

"Good for you." I finished reading the passage. "I think I'm beginning to see his point, and I'm not sure if I like it."

"Really?" Russ asked. "Enlighten me."

"Well, I keep approaching this thing with the government with a lot of anger and hatred."

"Yeah. Who wouldn't?"

"I don't know. But all I keep getting back is aggression and fear. Maybe I need to approach them with love?"

"Love the regulators?" Russ asked. "Have you lost your mind?"

"Maybe," I answered. "Or maybe all that I have to lose is a lot of fear and hatred." I paused for a moment, recollecting the dream. "The bear may have been the government, but I think that the spider was me."

"Okay," Russ said with an exaggerated sigh. "Let me guess. You didn't get much sleep last night."

"Very funny."

"How can the spider have been you? You were already there, remember?"

"It was a dream, Russ. We don't have to look at it literally. I got out an old book of Edgar Cayce's dream interpretations last night. He says that a spider represents a web or tangle of deceit that the dreamer has fallen into."

"Well, if your fight with the government isn't a tangle or a web, then I don't know what is," Russ replied. "What did he say about the skin melting off?"

"He didn't mention it," I answered. "It must not be a common dream occurrence."

Russ and I both laughed. "Well, for the sake of the rest of us, let's hope not."

"But I think that Tahkamenon addressed it."

"Oh you do, do you?" Russ said. "Funny, I don't recall your reading anything about melting skin."

"Sure I did," I answered, picking up the notebook and quoting from the passage. "That which is false will fall from your being." I closed the notebook and laid it back on my desk. "See what I mean?"

"Maybe. But the spider still seems creepy to me."

I did not pursue the dream any further. Russ saw it as clearly related to the battle with the government. And so did I, at least partially. It had been the same with my psychologist who was convinced that my earlier breakdown was directly a result of my work. And it was, but not completely. Same with the dream. The stress of my job was *an* answer, not *the* answer.

Russ and I finished our discussion, and I sat alone in my office, thinking of the months and years of fighting and manipulation. As I again opened the notebook and scanned the pages, certain words and phrases screamed for my attention. "You must embrace them, even those who do not yet see. Especially those who do not yet see."

"Can I do that?" I wondered. "Can I embrace the people who want to harm me?" More words flowed before my eyes. "Choose love. Test the path. I can never forsake you. Draw others to the warmth of the truth."

I thought again of the dream. It now intrigued more than frightened me. Maybe it did hold the answer to freeing me from this tangle that had encompassed my life. I thought of the bear, unleashed and isolated at the center of the field. He had been scared too. I was sure of that now. He too was forced to perform for the pleasure of the crowd. It was an insight that helped me see the regulators in a new light. I still detested their actions, but I thought more compassionately of their hearts.

And then there was the struggle itself. It had become the bane of my existence, but maybe it had a purpose in my life far beyond providing health-care coverage. Maybe healing wounds was within my destiny. My mind swirled with maybes. I closed the notebook to stop the clamor and tried to focus again on the business. But before I could put my thoughts to rest, I reopened the notebook and wrote:

> I look with great anticipation to the moment of truth—to the day that I no longer see you through the barriers of my fear. Have faith. I will know you in the darkness and in the light. Stand free of the shadows. Allow your being to resonate with the power of the truth.
>
> I will come to you in love and in understanding. In your presence, in the presence of the spirit, I will come to know myself.

The beauty of the message washed over me, the love, the unity, the belief. And with it, I experienced an unusual sense of relief. I was convinced that somewhere there was an answer—the answer to the dream, the answer to my apprehension. I wasn't sure what it was yet. I wasn't sure that I even knew the question.

But for the first time amid all of the questioning, I was convinced that the answer was out there. Or maybe in there. Or maybe both.

Chapter Eighteen

As disturbing as the dream had been, it helped me to focus on my fears. I knew that I was afraid of the government; its sheer size and power would frighten anyone. But if I feared going forward with the battle, I also feared pulling back. I feared disappointing others as well as myself. I feared failure. I feared change. As the message grew and competed for my attention, I feared that I was not worthy to fulfill the potential of the words. And as angry as I had been with Tahkamenon for suggesting it, I did fear my own desires. I feared choosing my own path.

Where could your heart go that your soul would not follow? Where can I lead you that your spirit has not already known? What is it you desire, in the quiet, in the darkness? Where do you find solace yet fear to explore?

Do you think for a moment that your dreams are in vain? That they are not true at all? Is there any greater fear than that your core has no substance? Or that it does have potential, and you lack the ability to bring it forth? What folly this fear, for you have more ability than you can ever imagine.

I understand wanting nothing more than to stop the fear. So you turn from your heart and the terror subsides. It may be rewarding to make the pain go away. But there is no greater pain than denying your heart.

I was still angry with Tahkamenon. I held him responsible for the fears I now had to face. And the more impossible the situation, the angrier I became, an anger that energized even as it consumed me. The contrast between the beauty of the message and the pain of my human existence tormented me. My job became too painful to bear.

It was not the amount of work or the intensity of the fight or the intimidation of the government that wore me down. It was my recognition that this was not my battle, that the road I was on was not of my own choosing. Still I could not step off without hurting people whom I cared for, without putting my family at risk, without facing the demons in my heart.

So I stayed angry for months, angry with my work, with Tahkamenon, with myself.

Do not berate yourself for your difficulty in accepting the truth. You have been taught to ignore it. You have been sanctioned for following your heart. But where has the fear taken you? Are you fulfilled as you sit here today reading these words and searching for meaning? The emptiness that you feel is understandable. It has been a logical progression. You now long for a spiritual one.

You continue to believe in that which does not exist. You search belongings for meaning, structures for security, food for pleasure. You use people as prizes, accumulations of money as proof of the integrity of your intentions. Yet these things prove little more than the depth of your distraction.

Do you want to truly impress someone? Be joyous. Express love. Speak only the truth. Vibrate with the intensity and perfection of your soul.

Do this and they will care little for your accumulations. Touch their hearts, and they will never forget. You will leave a remembrance of love and desire, absent of envy, vibrating with light.

Practice giving, not of your possessions or even of your time, but solely of yourself.

You hold the answer. Always filled with the capacity for love. Always with the ability to experience joy. If you deny this ability, you deny the integral nature of your soul. You deny your connection to the spirit. You deny your ability to love yourself.

Forget your insecurities. You do not create the meaning that generates from your being, yet you surround it. You animate it with your movement. All too often you distort its reflection. Still, the meaning remains, as does your ability to reflect it more clearly, to experience the joy of allowing its significance to permeate your thoughts and to guide your actions.

"Be joyous," I thought with a deep sense of sadness. The words seemed sarcastic as they stared at me from the page. Joy was so foreign a concept that the word itself seemed cruel, another iron dagger through an already breaking heart.

"Would you stop talking about truth and love and forgiveness and give me some real answers?" I screamed to Tahkamenon. "Why are you torturing me?" I demanded. "Why are you making my life miserable? Why are you inflicting such pain?"

Tahkamenon answered my questions with some questions of his own.

Why do you so fear that movement which will take you to a better place? Is it your desire to keep intact a safety net, an ability to say that your failure is not true because you did not truly care? And yet the failure is true, truer than you allow yourself to believe, not for the failure to accomplish but for failure to follow your path.

I say this with great certainty because otherwise there would be no issue, no failure to discuss. You fail only in pursuit of false dreams. You know this to be true but you have yet to accept. You have yet to immerse yourself in the meaning and significance of this statement. You have yet to allow your actions to follow your heart.

I sometimes startle at your inability to see that which lies so clearly before your eyes and within your heart. But I must remember your barriers. I can only factor their impact in theory as one who observes but does not experience. I judge the strength of your walls from their impact on the movements of your world.

I know your soul completely; your barriers I understand only through observation. You must forgive my impatience and accept the purity of my intentions. I, in turn, will forgive you your resistance. However, I will never accept your constraints as they are perceived and not real.

It is my purpose to lower the veil, to hold your hand in the darkness. To stay by your side until you have found the courage to see only the light, to vibrate only with the beauty of the truth.

Suspend yourself in this moment of existence, disorete from your surroundings, detached from the movements of the physical world. Allow yourself to know your soul truly, for its movement and its action.

Although the message could be painful, I continued to turn to the writing for solace. I continued to search each passage for hope.

You stand against the tide of humanity. Hold fast to your soul. Listen only to your heart, and the tide will be unable to shake your footing or drown out the message with its rush. And once you have allowed yourself to experience true power, even for a moment, you will fear less the next.

I do not say it will be easy. If you allow the fear to enter you may stagger in your step and then doubt the ability of love to carry you through. But remember always that the truth will not fail you, its power indestructible. You need only find a way to surround yourself in its presence, to infuse your being with its light.

I finished writing and scanned the pages. "The truth will not fail you." The statement seemed simple enough, but what was the truth? It was not a new question. I had asked many times before, but had yet to receive an answer.

I had thought about the truth a lot as I fought with the government, my world clouded with deception and hatred. Where did the truth lie in our ongoing debate? We certainly had not found it in the courtrooms. There we encountered only a manipulation of evidence, a distorted reflection of the truth.

The lawyers on both sides were extremely competent, which meant mainly that they had an ability to tailor the facts and circumstances into a course of events that added up to a case. And the judge, who sat and listened or read the briefs, saw not the truth but our conflicting creations of reality.

I felt sick and isolated as I worked on our case, realizing that truth was not obtainable through this process of justice. Even worse, I now knew that it was not even the goal. At my emptiest, I began to believe that truth did not exist, that everything was manipulation and deception. Right or wrong, good or bad, we perceived our lives through an incredible number of filters. How then could we ever trust in our own beliefs?

As I wrote to escape the pressure, Tahkamenon responded to the questions that permeated my life.

Truth bears little resemblance to the actuality that you have come to call truth. The fact that you are male or female, tall or short, young or old, may be actual, but it is not true as I have described it to you. These are facts, actualities, void of meaning. Truth is never such. Truth vibrates with meaning; it resonates with love.

I give you this distinction because it is critical to your understanding. Actuality may be confusing, always needing to be viewed from the perspective of the creator. But truth is constant. No need to question the motivation, to wonder at the intention. Because you are confused, you are unwilling to accept.

I speak to you in truth and you struggle to absorb the message into your factual world. And through this process of supposed validation, you weaken the message. You block the flow.

What better proof of the truthfulness of my voice than the impact it has on your soul? Has your heart asked for a measurement? Has your soul requested a picture to believe? If you eliminate the doubt, you have no need for proof. Yet to do so you must rid yourself of fear. Fall within the faith. Trust that you cannot be misled because the truth is yours, inherent in your being.

Who better to know it on impact, to immediately accept the authenticity as it touches close to your heart?

"But, Tahkamenon," I asked, "we have taught ourselves to accept so many things that are not real. How then do we find the ability to believe in our hearts?"

Because the heart has existed for eternity. These years of false belief are merely a complication. You must accept that the ability of the heart is limitless and eternal. You need only reconnect with an ability you always have possessed.

As I wrote these words and viewed the deception that surrounded me, an idea formed in my mind. An understanding that truth did exist but that it was not of this world. Here we have facts. Here we need proof. But we can never prove the truth because it cannot be contained in facts. It can only be known.

Truth can never exist in a courtroom. It can only exist in our hearts.

I had spent the last few years of my life trying to prove a case, desperately wanting to bring the truth to light. And here was the understanding that the truth could not to be proven. It was a revelation. It eased my emptiness. It altered my expectations. I learned to view the battle for what it was. And what it was not.

Take my hand. You struggle so with that which is innate. Close your eyes; experience your soul. Feel the love, the compassion. The joy is tangible, filled with light, vibrating with hope. Focus on the message, not the words. Remember the key is acceptance, not knowledge, not understanding.

You know with your brain, so filled with distraction. You accept only with your heart. Do you sense the purity of acceptance? The lack of conflict? Remember those moments in your life, both good and bad, that ended in acceptance. Was not the acceptance always a relief? Did not the weight drop from your shoulders even if the acceptance was of pain?

Tahkamenon was right. The acceptance did ease my emptiness, but it also made me question my motivations. If I was not searching for the truth, then what was it I continued to pursue? Recognition, vindication, vengeance? And which of these was great enough for the sacrifice I had made of my life?

I felt trapped as I asked myself these questions—trapped by my job, trapped by my fears. Every alternative seemed fraught with pain. Should I leave work and forsake a battle that I had worked so hard to pursue? Or should I stay and allow my world to be further defined by a fight that had lost much of its meaning? What were the repercussions? Could I choose and hold fast to my soul?

These questions haunted me. The harder I fought, the harder I worked, the louder they rang through my consciousness, demanding an answer, accepting nothing less than a truthful reply.

As always, you hold the answer. No display of force or amount of confinement is stronger than the power of the truth. Authenticity is explosive, breaking many barriers and creating an impenetrable force.

Who can hurt you if you remain authentic? Really hurt you? Damage your soul? Do you believe anyone has the power to do this? Even your enemies? Even yourself?

I think it impossible, for your soul is divine, a critical part of an infinite whole. No human can harm it, although many will try. They will build many walls and work to block all the light. They will try to leave you in the cold and the dark with an emptiness that has no bottom and a belief that you have no hope.

Still, your soul remains, forever a part of your being. So you need only remember to search for the light in the murky corners of your existence.

And once you focus fully on the truth, if even a thread, you will be energized by its very existence. You will experience the healing power of vibration and redis-cover the eternal connection that exists within the inner sanctum of your heart.

Each time I sat down to write, Tahkamenon questioned my fears. He was strong and encouraging, challenging my beliefs and healing my heart.

All that you fear is but an illusion. There is no fearing the truth. There is no avoidance in faith.

The harm that you imagine is not of the spirit. I do not deny its significance, only its relevance. You cannot value the truth until you cease to value the distortion. You must look past the reflections. You must focus on the source. You must pursue not fear but love. Does this movement bring joy? Is it free of doubt? Does it vibrate with life? If not, what does? I cannot tell you the answers. I only can beseech you to listen to that message which vibrates distinctly within your soul.

So you must ask with this step, with each step, do I take this with love or motivated by fear? And fear is far more deceptive than you may think. It wears many faces; it has many sources. Do you not see it in anger and greed, in doubt and deception, in jealousy and hate? And the walls that it builds are different in depth and cohesion, in age and in strength. Yet removal remains the same—with love and with faith. You remove the barriers only with acceptance of the truth.

As always, you hold the answer. What will it take before you are able to trust this, before you allow yourself to believe? Are you not motivated by joy? Then you must walk toward the light and not run from your fear.

The paths are many away from the shadows. They go in all directions, leading nowhere. Yet the path to the light is distinct. You will find it only with positive action. You find it only with the guidance of your heart.

As I questioned my own path and spoke directly with Tahkamenon, I gradually pulled away from Russ. For several months I struggled in silence, except for the ongoing dialogue with my heart.

Hold my hand. Allow me to speak directly to your soul. Suspend your reasoning and allow the melody to flow within your being. Only then will you understand. Feel the energy, the lightness of your existence. Shed your barriers and nothing will restrain your movement. Barriers that are mortal. Unable to withstand the direct confrontation with the heart. Unable to withhold a soul unless you give in to your fear.

You choose. A difficult choice I know, but worse not to make it. To live in the darkness, surrounded by your fear. To walk paths of others. To feel lost in the wilderness, unable to find your way home.

Stop running for a moment, for many moments, for a lifetime if that is what it takes. Listen. Be patient. You know the way home. The paths you took were human. They cannot stop you from your spiritual journey. They have delayed your movement but only to an insignificant degree.

Have faith. You will find your way home. You will come to accept the immortality of your being and embrace the beauty of your soul.

As the pressure overwhelmed me, I reached back to Russ, to ask his advice, to see what he thought of Ta-hkamenon's words. I told him that I had to do something, anything. I could no longer stay put. He was supportive but cautious. Just what was it that I proposed to do? How was I going to help support my family if I chose to leave my job? Valid questions to which I had no definite answers.

Brian wanted me to abandon the fight with the government, but he too was unclear as to how we would survive. We relied heavily on my income. I felt a tremendous responsibility to my children, to their comfort and security. Self-sacrifice was one thing, but I knew in my heart that making a change would entail much more than that.

I spoke with my children of both the sacrifice and my desire to follow my heart. They surprised me with their responses. They were willing to give up so much, their toys, their activities, even our home. They trusted that

Brian and I would care for them, that we would love them. They knew instinctively that possessions were less important than dreams. I filed away their responses, hoping I would have the courage to repeat them when they found their own paths and were ready to make their own way.

My children saw the decision with the clarity of innocence. And while I tried to discount their perspective, I knew that it was my own that was tainted. Brian supported me. My children supported me. In an effort to support the book, Russ and Mary Ellen were willing to bear some of the risk. I was free to decide. I realized then that no matter the depth of my fears, I had always possessed a choice.

But what was it that I wanted, truly, without the need for coercion, with only the guidance of my heart?

You recognize the walls; now break down the barriers. They are more difficult to live with than without. The message is your safety net. Fall within the light. Experience the joy of freeing your soul from the confines of your doubt.

If only you could see from here, but you can do even better; you can see from your soul, you can act from your heart. You need only tear down the walls that have restrained your movement. You have created them. You have allowed them. At times you have even welcomed their existence. Now you must remove them. You must allow your soul to guide your movement.

I did not yet know what I wanted, but of one thing I was perfectly clear. I could not find the quiet to listen amid the turmoil of my job and the needs of my family. My family I had chosen. My job—it had just happened. I had given it my heart and my soul. I now needed to reclaim them.

I still did not know where I was going, but now more than ever I was determined to find my way. The next morning as I drove to work, my mind consumed with the choices that lay before me, I came to an overpass, flooded with sunlight, and heard undeniably the voice of Tahkamenon.

> Well, Mrs. Wilkinson, you shall have all of the answers to the questions you choose to ask. The universe has opened her arms, and you, my dear child, have opened your heart.

The message was calling. My soul was responding. My heart pounded relentlessly against my chest. Tahkamenon had expressed his undeniable support. So I placed one foot upon my path. It was a tentative step at best. I could not find it within myself to leave my job completely, but I did cut my hours in half and focused more energy on the book. I risked telling people about it. More than ever before, I put my beliefs on the line. I committed to exposing my dreams, my heart, myself.

I thought again of my dream and my fears and the spider. I closed my eyes and watched as he leapt through the air, his skin melting away. I thought of Tahkamenon. "That which is false will fall from your being." I summoned my courage and chose to leap forward, to face my fears and follow my heart.

It was, without a doubt, a most terrifying choice.

Chapter Nineteen

Having chosen to focus on the book, I now actively pursued both the words and their significance. I wanted to hold the message in my heart and feel it and live it and share it with others. I questioned myself carefully. What steps should I take? What were my desires? What was it that I had to give?

In response I wrote clearly of my path and my choices, of my intentions and my goals. It began with a unique passage, at Tahkamenon's inspiration, but clearly in my own voice.

> This is the path that I have chosen with my heart and my soul. It is a message that speaks to my being without the pressures of the world. For no reason other than the light. I know this as the truth. Not because I speak it but because it flows from the heart, my heart, many hearts. It needs not validation, each word proof of the truthfulness of the whole.

I will find a way to reach others. To knock on the door of their many walls and ask that they allow the melody entry, that for only a moment they suspend the fear of many lifetimes and allow themselves to believe. Not for me nor for any other reason than the profound effect it will have upon their souls.

And with that crack they will glimpse the limitless potential of living within the flow of the melody instead of within the confines of the walls. This is my hope—to allow each person that moment. So that their hearts may be opened to their own connections. So that these words may remind them of the melody that exists always within.

There was a break in the writing and I wrote as if in response.

These words are mere representations, but they are the best I can do given my current limitations of expression and yours of acceptance. We will get better with time, the words less necessary. But for now we must find a broader means of communication.

I stopped again and read this new paragraph. I then smiled at Tahkamenon and responded:

And so we have this—words that follow my heart as closely as my ability allows.

So there it was. My commitment. The answer to what I wanted, the clues to my path. I wanted to bring this message to others, to use my words to touch their hearts. I accepted the responsibility of sharing the message and continued exploring my soul.

There is no truth that is not motivated by love and perceived with love. Without love this message would be heresy. Each person must perceive it with love for the words to ring with true meaning. It is a joint effort, a multiple effort, enhanced by each individual who accepts the message within his heart.

I had been searching for truth and now I felt closer. It could only exist in the absence of fear and the presence of love. It was another important discovery. Russ and I could not speak the truth, not completely. We could only speak from our hearts and trust that others would listen with theirs.

But what was love? If we found truth elusive, then love was impossible to define.

What is love? I sense such fear in your question, such apprehension in your heart? What irony, accepting both fear and hatred and wary of the power of love.

You have practiced distortion with no greater persistence than with this emotion that defines your existence as both human and spirit. You have distorted it with fear and used its beauty to exploit others, all the while unknowingly exploiting yourself. Of course you have not distorted love, only your perception. Yet even this distortion has been enough to cause a great deal of confusion, to instill a great deal of pain.

Love is of the spirit, but so much of what you feel, so much of what you believe yourself to be, is controlled not by love but by fear. And fear is of your world only, a by-product of your walls.

You hold each other not out of love but insecurity, each failing to recognize the distortion. Or at least you do not acknowledge it, hoping that it will get better, that one day love will fulfill its promise and bring you closer to peace. But that can never happen until you learn to face the fear, until you confront the distortion and eliminate it from your heart.

Yet for all of its distortion on your physical plane, love remains a source of tremendous power, a promise of eternal hope.

A tremendous power. An eternal hope. Love was that and so much more. As the days progressed, Russ and I discussed love quite a bit. We contemplated its impact and wrote of its beauty.

My love for you is endless, expanding to fill each crevice that you allow yourself to reveal. Try to imagine the boundaries of your own love. Is this possible or are you beginning to comprehend the limitless, borderless expression of the spirit? Love has no boundaries. Focus on this. Concentrate fully on the feeling of love.

What I say is less foreign than you have allowed yourself to believe. You already know the experience of moments without boundaries, of feeling void of walls. Of course you call many things love, yet you recognize the deception in your heart.

Remember those moments of true love, stray as wildflowers in the open fields of your life. Imagine this moment, filled with that beauty, bursting in color and fragrance and joy. Imagine each moment, one after another, vibrating with the intensity of the fields and the warmth of the sun. Imagine a moment, an hour, a day. Imagine a lifetime. Imagine the spirit, an eternity of love, an eternity of moments too beautiful to describe as the beauty is in the vibration and the warmth and the power of emotions untainted by pain.

And when your heart falters, your mind exploding with effort, go back to a moment of singular joy. A single moment that holds the answer to eternity past and eternity present. A single heart that for one precious moment allowed itself to experience love.

And if that moment is possible, then so is a lifetime.

Russ and I decided to share our love with others, to consciously find ways to bring more love into our world.

It is true that you must love yourself before you love others, because only within can you find the authenticity of feeling that we have come to call love. Only inside can you find the connection that is based solely on love. Only from within can you reach out and touch the heart of another.

Loving those we cared about seemed easy. But what about everyone else? How were we to embrace those who angered us, who frightened us, who seemed intent on inflicting pain? And yet these seemed to be the very people that we needed to love the most. We began to recognize the risk we associated with this emotion and our resistance to its force.

Love is a powerful emotion. There is none truer in your life. Yet you fear its tumultuous impact. But the turmoil is caused by fear not love. And the only way to overcome the fear is to have faith in the loving, to believe in your heart, to hold closely to the vibrations of your soul.

Hate may seem consuming but nothing matches the power and significance of love. Hate creates barriers; love transcends them. And love produces joy—a universal message of smiles and laughter.

So love and truth were related, one dependent on the other. And both were critical in overcoming our fears. To find the truth, we must first make choices with love in our hearts. Then the fear will subside if we continue to trust in our strength and find the courage to believe in our souls.

> Take this step. Choose love if only for a moment. Practice on others. Practice on yourself. Find a ray of light and focus your energy to expanding its presence. Build a bridge. Tear down a wall. Hold the hand of another and open your soul. Try with all of your being to act in accordance with your heart.

> Just for this instance; just for this moment. Do not create an expectation for the next. Allow it to flow naturally. Do not berate yourself for falling away from the love, for clouding its presence with reflections of fear.

"Choose love," I thought as I read this passage. "If only for a moment." How beautiful. What an incredibly wonderful choice. What a gift to understand that love didn't just happen but that it was a decision we each could make. One we could choose moment by moment and lifetime by lifetime. It made sense. Some people seemed surrounded with love and others removed. But love wasn't more available to some than others. It was more chosen. It was more cherished. It was more accepted.

> Each moment is unique in its potential, the culmination of eternity past meeting the unlimited hope of eternity future. The spirit exists in this moment, vibrating and full of life. What a miracle this moment. Can you imagine a more precious gift? Yet it is yours for the taking, just for the living, a lifetime of possibility. Each moment is reason to hope. The key—to fill each one with love.

As the message became more real in our lives, Russ and I viewed our surroundings with clarity. We thrilled at the abundance; we despaired at the pain. We felt each more intensely. Our hearts rejoiced at acts of kindness and ached with the suffering that surrounded us. We marveled at the misery we inflict on each other, on those that we know and those that we pretend to love.

We wrote more precisely about the purpose of love and tried to carry the concepts into our actions and into our world.

> What is the destruction of the family if not a destruction of yourselves? Can you abandon your children and not your souls? A bond for each other that defies physical separation, a joining of the hearts. Are you beginning to understand? This is the message. You are bound one to another. You cannot sever the ties without harming yourselves. The pain of separation reminds you that the bond was meant to be. Separate you may find distraction, but you will never know peace.

> Some breakdown is necessary. Your borders are arbitrary. You are being made to understand the value of commitment, the impenetrable nature of spiritual bonds. Do not limit your family by definition. Kinship knows no genealogical bounds. You are connected from the source and in the source. You cannot restrict your love or your loyalty, for each person that you remove from the circle cuts you off from a valuable piece of yourself.

I sent this passage to Russ and we spoke on the phone. "Do you think that we'll ever learn?" I asked. "That with all of this anger and violence and hatred . . . will we ever understand that we're only hurting ourselves?"

"I hope so," Russ answered. "I guess that's the goal. But it's so easy to hate, so much harder to love. That must be our humanness."

"It's not our humanness," I responded. "It's our delusion. It's the price that we pay for our walls."

A few days later, Russ sent me a passage of his own.

Do you understand then that the need for community is not about security? It's about the expansion of love. What better example than your family? A child is born of his mother and father and by that birth community and communal love is born. Call the aunts. Call the uncles, the cousins, the loved ones, the friends. Behold someone else to love. Behold someone else to love us. Thus community is born, not of walls or of rules but of love.

Understand that this is what mankind is to be about. Color, race, religion, origin, and sex must be communized until each is unrecognizable. And then your walls of hate will melt into tears of joy. Behold love. Behold each other. Feel it in your being. Expand it to the universe.

Imagine a million people, neighbors, in a community where they collectively experience love and share that love with the universe. Imagine the power. Imagine the impact—on the million, on us all. Would it not be more than a million times one but the power of a million million? An exponential experience.

That is what universal love is all about. That is what God is all about—the collective consciousness of all those who are capable of love, loving on this plane, accepting this love in their lives. Imagine a planet of beings, exceeding the boundaries of this planet, extending their love into the universe, receiving this love in their hearts.

This has been tried in other places but has yet to be realized. It is why each and every one of you has chosen to come to this place in time. Each person has chosen to be part of the growth, to nurture the transformation and the expansion of this force into the universe.

I read Russ's passage and thought of my father-in-law, Ken. Before his death, he had been a rural sociologist who had stood among his scientific peers and proclaimed that they could not study community without considering the impact of love. He understood its magnitude. He believed in its power. These words evoked his memory, his concept of community, his belief in the significance of love.

Community is part of the puzzle of universal love. You each have come to see the picture on the box and were distracted by the array of illusions. Still, you recognize the picture. You know the way home when you light upon the path.

It is a picture that is best comprehended through multiple eyes, best understood through multiple souls. It is the reason for your separateness on this planet. But it in no way diminishes your oneness. You must hold both simultaneously. Believe in your purpose. Accept the connection.

Love is the key. You are neighbors, one in the universal community, of one source, returning to that place that each of you knows in your distant memory to be your home.

"Where is home?" I wondered, as I read these words and continued to search for my own direction. I understood in my heart where I was going but I still wondered at each step. I questioned my choices and listened closely to my soul.

It is something to be understood in this lifetime, that you are descending a mountain, heading home. All journeys are circular. Inevitably you return to the source. Home is not a physical experience. It is a return to the spirit. It is a return to yourself.

Russ and I continued on our journey, both individually and together, with a renewed sense of purpose and a clear sense of direction. We each felt distinctly the stirrings of our hearts.

I know not where we go from here. But the movement continues and I sense the vibration in the distance. It will be the return—the moment of recognition, viewing your home in the distance, saturated with clarity and under-standing.

We rejoiced in the beauty of the message. Even with the distractions and deception of our world, we were find-ing a way to reach out to others, to carry love in our hearts. We chose love in our meetings, in our conversa-tions, in our confrontations. It was an incredible change. Not everyone responded at first, but slowly the anger and the meanness just slipped away. There was no room left when we filled our spaces with love.

This is a critical moment in your life, in the life of the spirit. Experience the energy of finding your own true path, of releasing your fear, of basking in the light. Experience the synergy of moving into alignment with the collective consciousness of the spirit. Feel the ex-hilaration of running through the fields, surrounded by the blur of color, the wind kissing your cheeks, the sun warming your back. Notice the lightness of your step. Fear is much heavier than faith. It carries many walls, much weight upon your soul.

So you've broken through the barriers and come to believe that gravity has more to do with fear than with physics, that only your doubt restrains you from your flight into eternity.

There is so much to be experienced. Infuse your life with meaning. Immerse your heart in love.

The message continued to flow in its beauty, each word and each sentence filling our hearts with its warmth. It was a beautiful moment in our lives, filled with possibility, expectation, and hope.

In the end, you find truth, you find each other, you find security, you find home, you find harmony, you find the spirit, you find yourself, with love.

We were finding ourselves, thrilling at the recognition of our hearts. Holding our souls as if by the hand and stepping through our lives with desire, not motivated by fear or driven by habit. We thanked Tahkamenon for the beauty he had brought to our lives. More than anything else, we thanked him for returning us to our source.

I see you now clearly. I see myself. Faith exists no longer. Nor does fear. This is truth. This is acceptance. This is love.

Chapter Twenty

The steps gained momentum, one right after another, each movement pushing forward the next. Russ and I cherished the opening of our souls. Our lives changed, not our surroundings but our perception. We saw everything differently. We experienced joy.

As if by magic, new people appeared in our lives at just the right moment, offering encouragement and wisdom that inspired us to proceed with the book. Within days of reducing my hours at work, I met Doug MacKinnon through a mutual friend. Doug was a lobbyist and a nationally syndicated columnist, who was about to publish his first novel. For no other reason but kindness, he graciously took Russ and me under his wing.

After our first meeting, Doug requested a formal book proposal to circulate in the industry—another incredible opportunity. But preparing a proposal meant that we had to decide on the format. We could no longer waiver. We had to make a decision, and we had to do it now.

Russ scheduled a visit so that we could sit down together

and reach a consensus. He arrived, and we sat at my dining room table with notepads in front of us and a stack of our writing in between.

Before we launched into a discussion over format, I pulled a crumpled piece of paper from the stack. "You're never going to believe what I found the other day."

"The Holy Grail?" Russ asked, raising his eyebrow.

"Is that what we've been looking for?" I replied, as I flattened out the paper with the palm of my hand. "You really should have told me before now."

"Kind of," he answered. "Now, what did you find?"

"This," I said, dangling the paper in front of his face. "*The* list."

"What list?" Russ asked as he snatched it from my hand. He sat for a moment reading the words. "What is this?"

"It's your list."

"My list? What the hell are you talking about? It's your handwriting."

"That's because I took notes," I said. I took the list back from Russ. "This is what you originally told me about your discussions with Tahkamenon."

"And you took notes?" Russ asked in amazement. "And then saved them? Do you keep everything?"

"Only things that matter."

"And this mattered?"

"Of course it mattered. This list is what inspired me to write the first passage, the one about you and Tahkamenon. Or me and Tahkamenon," I added, confused by my own statement.

Russ took back the paper and read the list again. "So this is what I told you?" he said, leaning back in his seat. "And you still decided to work with me?"

"Pretty amazing, isn't it?"

Russ stared out the window as he spoke. "Sort of but not really. Certainly not any more amazing than all of the other unbelievable things that have happened between us." He turned and looked at me directly. "I told you that it was unbelievable, you know, right from the very beginning."

"I know, I know," I responded, rolling my eyes. We sat and stared at each other in silence. "But it's only unbelievable in our minds," I added. "We've never doubted any of this with our hearts."

"You win," Russ said and smiled. "It certainly has always been believable in our hearts."

Russ turned back to the list and read aloud, "'Religion is with purpose, without rules.' That pretty much sums up what we wrote about religion, doesn't it?"

"Yeah," I responded. "Tahkamenon has said many things about religion, but he never disputed its purpose, only the rules that would exclude individuals from their source."

"I don't think that we can really exclude anyone," Russ said. "We may think so. But no matter our perception, we don't have the power to cut people off from their souls."

"We've sure made quite an industry out of convincing people that we can," I replied.

"Yeah," Russ laughed. "And then telling them that we can reconnect them with God. But only if they do what we say."

"You've got to admit, it's a powerful way to do business."

"Sure is," Russ responded, as he again scanned the list in his hands. "Oh, I remember this conversation," he said. "That man has created nothing. I was angry when Tahkamenon first said it. I mean we had created lots of things—buildings, clothing, computers, light. But he laughed when I suggested this. 'It's not creation,' he said. 'It's rearrangement. And you haven't created light,' he added. 'You may harness it, like you harness energy. But you do not create it.'" Russ suddenly burst out laughing himself.

"What's so funny?" I asked.

"Nothing really. Just how much angrier I was when I realized that he was right."

"Oh, I don't know that we haven't created anything," I said. "Even Tahkamenon says that we've created hunger, poverty, emptiness."

"Maybe he meant that we haven't created anything of value."

"That's pretty pessimistic," I replied.

"Not really," Russ answered. "I think his point is that our value is not in what we've built or harnessed or accumulated. Our value is eternally embedded in our souls."

I took the list from Russ. "What about 'convergent paths'? We've written a lot about finding our own paths but not about convergent ones."

"Indirectly," Russ said. "Remember, 'we will go individually and together.' And he's spoken often of our collective consciousness."

"That's true," I replied. "And if we are all of one source and we each are returning home, then I guess, by default, our paths will converge."

"What about this last one?" Russ asked, looking over my shoulder. "'Thirteen minus seven equals six.' Now there's some insight for you."

"It could be," I answered. "Who knows, it could represent linear thought. You know, all that is linear can only be added together or taken away. Or it could be an example of a fact that bears little meaning in isolation." I paused and smiled at Russ. "Or it could be that you mixed up Autumn's homework with your Tahkamenon writing. It's pretty much a toss-up for me."

"No, it was much more than that. I remember—it was one of the conversations that I understood completely at the moment, blown away by its impact, and then could never fully recover. I was just left with the essence."

"Or at least with thirteen minus seven equals six," I said and laughed.

"Go to hell," Russ responded. "Not everything you say is exactly earth-shattering either."

"Did you say earth-shattering?" I asked. "Well look, we've got that right here on this little old list too. 'Ability is only to destroy planet not souls.'" I placed the list back on the stack of paper. "I don't think Tahkamenon would say it that way, though. It seems a bit negative for him."

"Well, it's obviously been through a few translations. And we certainly have written a great deal about our human frailty—our bodies, our walls, our world."

"And the indestructibilty of our souls," I added. "Remember what he said. 'You are divine, your soul protected.' Isn't that cool?"

"Way cool," Russ responded, as we turned together to sort through the stack of writing between us.

I flipped through the pages without seeing them, trying to find the courage to tell Russ my plan. I did not know why I was afraid. It made perfect sense. But I knew that what I was thinking was a dramatic change from anything we had ever discussed.

"What if we didn't mention Tahkamenon?" I finally asked, as we continued to sort through the passages.

"To whom?" Russ asked, not looking up from the papers.

"In the book," I said. "What if we didn't mention him in the book?"

"What, are you crazy?" Russ laid down the papers and turned in his seat.

"No. I'm serious." He looked as if he was about to say more but I held up my hand. "Just wait. I've been thinking about this a great deal. Just listen to what I have to say."

"Okay," Russ said, folding his arms across his chest. "I'm listening."

"Well, it's just all been so confusing. There's you. There's me. There's Tahkamenon." I stopped for a moment and rubbed my hands down the stack of writing. "And then there's this—this beautiful message, these powerful words. And the message is what it really is all about. So why not focus only on the message? We can incorporate these words and these ideas into a third party observation on life and our existence." I stopped talking and Russ was silent. "Are you mad?" I asked.

"Not mad," he answered. "Surprised. I mean I never considered that we would do this without Tahkamenon."

"We're not doing it *without* Tahkamenon," I said. "It's all based on him, on his message. But if we use his name, then we have to explain who he is." Tears welled in my eyes. "I want to reach out to people with these words. I want to touch their hearts." I closed my eyes and took a deep breath. "I'm afraid that if we say we're talking with a spirit, no one will bother to read the rest."

Russ rubbed his forehead with both hands. "Okay," he said, leaning forward to brush a tear from my cheek. "We can certainly try it. I mean it's not like I have some other brilliant idea about how to pull this all together."

I grabbed a Kleenex and concentrated on stopping my tears. "We also wouldn't have to write about ourselves like Joe suggested," I added. "You know that we couldn't figure out what to say anyway."

"We're really not going to mention Tahkamenon at all?" Russ asked.

"In the acknowledgments," I answered. "We'll thank him for his guidance, for his insight. And if we do make this book work, then someone is eventually going to ask us where these thoughts came from." I crumpled up the Kleenex and threw it in the trash. "But then they'll be asking. Then they'll be less likely to turn away when we tell them the truth." Russ still looked uncertain. "Trust me," I pleaded. "Just give me a chance."

Russ smiled. "Did you ever doubt that I would?"

"Only for a moment," I said, smiling in return. "Oh, and you can't write any more passages."

"What?" Russ shrieked. "Are we not putting the writing in the book either?"

"No. Calm down. Of course we are putting the writing in the book. The writing *is* the book. But if we keep adding to the writing, I'll never be able to finish the book." I leaned over and touched Russ's hand. "Look, I'm sorry. You can write all you want. And keep talking to Tahkamenon. I just meant that I need to cut off what we're going to include."

"Any more *rules* I should be aware of?" Russ asked.

"No," I answered, ignoring his tone. "I think that just about covers it."

So it was settled. We would write the book without needing to explain Tahkamenon. Or our connection. Or who we were. It would be only message, purely message. Later we could tell the whole story.

Finally, I was convinced that we had found a format that worked.

Chapter Twenty-One

After we decided on the format, the process went smoothly. We sorted the passages by main ideas and started to weave them together. We wrote the proposal as we went along, outlining the book and completing a few sample chapters to include with our submission. It was strange not referring to Tahkamenon or to ourselves, but it was certainly simpler. It was definitely less of a risk.

As soon as we had completed the proposal, we sent it to Doug for his review. He responded with enthusiasm, another wonderful display of support. Doug added a personal letter and forwarded the proposal to his agent. Russ and I did our best to wait patiently for a response.

We continued to work on the book as we waited, writing more chapters and refining the outline. When we had not received a reply within a few months, our frustration and our fear grew with each passing day.

Then it happened—we received a rejection. Although very unusual for the industry, it was a personalized letter that actually critiqued our work. The agent had been impressed by both the message and the writing but felt that we needed to be noted spiritual leaders to make the book a success.

"See, Tahkamenon. What did I tell you?" I said, laughing at the irony. I initially had been so convinced that we needed credentials. Although I now knew differently, it was only fitting that our first rejection should be the actualization of my fear.

I called Russ to break the news. "I've decided to start a cult," I said when he answered. "I've already been going door-to-door in my neighborhood, and this is actually a lot easier than I would have thought."

"Oh really. May I ask why?"

"I got the letter today. The book's great, but the agent thinks that we need to be spiritual leaders in order to sell it."

"Well, you are, aren't you? I mean that's always how I describe you to my friends. 'You know my friend Val, the spiritual leader.'"

"Maybe I can just make up a business card—Valerie L. Wilkinson, Noted Spiritual Leader."

"And you have to start wearing flowing dresses," Russ said. "Preferably something gauzy and white. Hey, read me the letter," he added.

So I did. As much as we tried to make light of it, we were very disappointed. We knew the statistics. We understood that we were trying to beat incredible odds. But everything had fallen into place so perfectly that we could not help but hope that this first submission would work.

The disappointment intensified as the days progressed, as we told everyone about it, as we tried to explain that this was the normal course of events. The more that we said, the more that we doubted, the more that we questioned whether this book was really meant to be.

The changes will be many before you have fully accepted the truth. This is still but a beginning. Traveling across the expanses, you will shed many barriers, eclipse many constraints, wonder at the freedom of your movement, and come suddenly upon new walls previously hidden from your view. And just as before, you may not recognize them as constraints until the movement wells up against the unyielding forces, until the comfort is replaced by the terror of confinement.

And so again the need to give up that which is familiar, that which has brought you forward to this moment. There will be much breaking through. Do not be discouraged. Each time will be easier, more filled with light, less tinged with pain, until finally you rejoice at the barriers, each an opportunity to attain a new level.

"The need to give up that which is familiar?" I asked when I read the passage. "Hadn't I given up enough?" I wondered. I had cut my hours in half. I had laid myself on the line. I had focused my energy on the writing. What more did he want? What more did I have to give?

How many times must you feel the breaking of your heart before you allow your feet to walk new paths? How much pain, created by your actions, intensified by your fear, must you experience before you allow yourself to listen? Before you find the courage to release the walls and allow the bricks to crumble from the pressure of their own collective weight?

"What walls are you talking about now?" I asked. As much as I believed that I had addressed my own fears and faced my own walls, I could not dismiss these words as nonsense. Everything that Tahkamenon had said, every fear that he had questioned, had turned out to be true.

"What are we missing?" I wondered. "What piece of the puzzle have we failed to comprehend?"

> There are no distinctions in the truth. It is absolute and all encompassing. All are welcome to join us on the path. Eventually each will find his way. The collective movement will help those who falter against the weight of their own fear, of all of our fears.

> Have faith. You need not struggle so with the truth. Open your eyes. Listen with your heart. You feel the difference. You understand when you light upon the path. Now it is upon you to align your actions with these moments of insight, these flashes of inspiration. And that is the easier part of the task. The harder by far is to stop the action not dependent on these moments; the movement set in motion years ago, deflected by the walls, driven by the habit.

Hadn't we aligned our actions with our insights? Russ and I had worked hard on the book. We had developed the proposal. We had reached out to others. We each carried love in our hearts. What more did it take to move into alignment? What movements remained a result of our walls?

The walls now confused me. For so long I had felt the movement, the freeing motion of my heart. Yet now I stood alone in the darkness, unable to decipher the path, confronted with barriers I had thought would fall easily. Isn't that what Tahkamenon told me? That the movement would get easier? That the walls would fall faster? That eventually I would walk solely in the light?

> Ah, but you do walk easier, with deeper comprehension of your movement, with more acceptance of your path. You are already forgetting the emptiness of disbelief. It

is not easy, walking the line between parallel worlds. That which is human longs for distraction, for definition, for tangible signs and colorful words. That which is spirit focuses wholly on the light, listens solely to the message, follows only one true path.

On your planet, within the context of your lifetime, it is the human that is both seen and heard. Therefore it is the human that must be very quiet for that which is spirit to be known.

Focus on the quiet. Try to create an extended moment of stillness in your soul. Then you will again feel the movement—the stirring deep within your being, the movement of the universe, the echoes of your heart.

Allow yourself to experience the moment without rushing to partake. There is plenty of time for running. For now, permit yourself to enjoy the beauty of knowing that you are about to follow your own true path. Make ready again for the journey. You have done so before and will do so again. Each time carries you closer to the center, deeper within yourself.

Hold on to the connection. Allow it to energize your being. Sway with the vibration. Listen to the music. Trust that you will move when you are ready and, at that moment, the universe will be ready for your movement.

"What movement is he waiting for?" I asked Russ when I showed him this passage. "If he would tell me, I would take it. I feel like we're back to square one."

"Don't worry," Russ said. "It will happen. This is only one rejection. We just need to move forward. We will publish the message. We will find someone to publish this book."

Each step is not predestined, only the path, only the return to the source. You will experience many changes in your perception. You will come to experience light, to move with the rhythm of the universe, to flow with the water, to accept the truth.

This is not a linear experience. You try to make it so and wonder at your frustration. You try to hold onto the pretext of the physical world as you analyze the spiritual. Neither will work, not the prism of your plane nor the application of your intellect.

This is about being, not about explaining. It is about experiencing the light, not about seeing it. It is about knowing the truth, not about proving it. It is about love. It is about forgiveness. It is about the oneness that surrounds you, never letting go even as you struggle with distinction, even as you hate and harm and belittle. Even as you imagine others better or worse. Even as you believe that forgiveness has to do with anyone else but yourself.

Hold on to the oneness. Look through the distinctions of your world. Come to understand that they are merely an illusion. You may enjoy them but not believe them. For in the belief, in the vesting of power, you will have turned away from the truth.

"I haven't turned away from anything," I pleaded. "And what do you mean about forgiveness? Who is it that I have to forgive?" Just weeks ago, the message had been so clear. I was living it. I understood it. What could have happened? How could I now be so confused?

While I tried to rationalize this latest obstacle, I again confronted the limitations I had placed on my life. I still tried to pretend that my barriers were external, but I knew, without question, that they were of my own making. I had created them, and I had allowed them, if not with my consent then with my silence.

As I questioned the role that I played in the creation of walls, Tahkamenon spoke gently, supporting my questions, encouraging my thoughts.

It was meant to be this moment, encapsulated by the physical world. Experience the vastness of the spirit as it struggles against the confinement, strengthening the connection by pushing at the edges. I am proud of your journey, of your ability to continue onward, of your realization that the physical world does not generate the meaning that you long to experience.

Do not let fear restrain you. Start not with the fears of others but with your own. What is that which you fear most? What are the movements that you make in your life, driven by that fear? What walls have you built? To what degree do they constrain your movement?

For some reason, I kept thinking about my job as I read these passages and searched for answers. While I had focused more on the book, I had not released my emotional connection to my work. I was still caught up in the battle, and it became more difficult with every passing day. One obstacle followed another, one disappointment only led to the next.

Nothing true is impossible. You fail only in pursuit of false goals. You fail only when your actions are disharmonious, when you restrict your soul from singing freely. So what of such failure? It is to be valued for it teaches a lesson if you are willing and ready to learn. The failure is not in your abilities, which are endless, but in your choice.

"'You fail only in pursuit of false goals.' Is that what this is about?" I wondered. "Is my job holding me back from fulfilling my heart?" Tahkamenon kept talking about movement. Maybe leaving completely was the one move that I had to find the courage to make.

Before long, I did. I faced my own fear of quitting and everyone else's of abandonment. I did not want to run, not from the battle or the government or the pressure. But I knew that I was not running away. I was running forward. I was following my heart.

Once I left work, Russ and I turned up the intensity on the book. We rewrote the proposal. We studied the industry and submitted letters to agents and publishers alike. The odds of rejection were astronomical. We read the statistics against us without acknowledgment. We had committed to Tahkamenon. The message was too important. We could no longer allow our fear to hold us back.

Soon the responses started flowing—incredible reactions to the beauty of the message. Handwritten letters and personalized statements that clearly indicated a favorable response to the words. But there was no acceptance. We still had not found a way to publish the book.

I dealt continually with my own impatience, feeling the void in my life more acutely and watching as I rushed in circles to erase its existence. I wanted beyond anything to rid myself of the sadness and fill the empty spaces of my soul.

Your soul is not empty. It is fuller than you have imagined but not too full for you to experience. You must move past the pain. You must follow your heart. You must face your fear. Fully, honestly, with love. Not defiance. That will not work. But with courage. The courage to take your fear by the hand and walk your path side by side, to experience it until it is known. And once known, the fear will fade, slipping through your fingers like so many granules of sand. For its power was in its imagined potential. Not in its truthfulness. Not in its light.

I love you. You seem so fragile in your human form, yet I know fully of your strength. Your humanness cannot diminish the power of your soul. Still the struggle for alignment weighs upon your being. This would not be if you would allow yourself to follow your heart.

I wanted to experience a life run by the calling of my heart, to make decisions based on desire, not fear. I wanted to dispose of those actions and routines in my life carried out only for the purpose of placating others. It was not that I did not love many deeply. It was only that I could not serve them fully if I did not first serve myself. I wanted these things. And I felt that I was pursuing them. I could not understand what it was that now stood in our way.

These words and this message so easy to hear yet difficult to comprehend, to implement in your lifetime, to enact in your world. It shouldn't be this difficult, and the time will come when it will not be so. But for now you must break the restraints of the barriers and halt the momentum of your lives. You may wonder why you are the ones, but it has been a continuum and this is your moment. The message may seem a revelation, but it is no more so than the many that have come before and are now such a part of your consciousness that you fail to comprehend the radical nature of the change which they initially represented.

So too it will be with this message. Radical for some, logical for others, it will become with time an assumption. No one will question your unity, your divinity, your source. You will find honor in love much more so than hatred, fulfillment in peace much more so than war. This moment all the better for the knowledge that it will become commonplace. The pain of tearing down the walls all the easier with the hope that fewer and fewer will be built. The beauty of the garden all the more vibrant for the warmth of the light and the proliferation of love.

We continued with the submissions, and the rejections kept filing in. They were filled with encouragement but included little specific information. Always there was the indication that the concept was wonderful, the message was powerful, but something was "just not quite right."

After months of trying on our own, Russ and I decided that it was time to go back to Joe and Ruth for their insight. I met with Ruth and gave her the proposal. She read a few pages when we were together and seemed impressed with the organization and touched by the words. She took the proposal home and promised to get back to me soon with her comments.

I looked forward to her remarks. We had put in a great deal of work, and I felt confident of her response.

Chapter Twenty-Two

Ruth handed me the sealed envelope with hesitation. I knew immediately that she did not want me to look inside until she left. "Oh my God," I thought as I looked in her eyes. "She hates it." I was devastated. She had seemed so interested before, but now I sensed only her fear.

I drove home with the envelope lying on the seat beside me. I decided to wait and read what she had written in the comfort of my home. "What could have gone wrong?" I wondered, hating myself for failing to portray the beauty of Tahkamenon's words. It had to be me. I had failed. I had seen it in her eyes.

Once home, I settled into my chair and opened the envelope. "First, I wouldn't change a thing right now," the letter started. "Okay," I thought, "so maybe she doesn't hate it, but something is bothering her."

I scanned the letter looking for the answer. It jumped at me from the middle of the page: "Why is this woman, who I know to be courageous, so afraid to tell the true story?"

"Bitch," I responded without hesitation. "What does she mean 'afraid'? I *am* telling the truth. Didn't she read the proposal? The truth is what this whole book is about." My thoughts swirled and blood rushed to my face. I stood and paced the room as I read the letter from start to finish. I wanted to scream as I took in the words. She was questioning my courage. Me—the woman who was willing to take on the federal government, the one who dealt with regulators one-on-one and who refused to succumb to their intimidation. How could she possibly question my courage? Screw her.

"She doesn't even know what she's talking about," I thought. "I'm not afraid to tell the story of Tahkamenon or tell people about my connection to Russ. We are doing it this way so that people will listen. So that they won't read the word 'spirit' and turn away from the message. We want this to be about the message not about us. We'll tell that story later. She just doesn't understand."

I picked up the phone and called Russ. He wasn't at the office so I tracked him down in his car. I tried to control my anger. In all fairness, Ruth had said several positive things about the proposal. She definitely still believed in the book. It took courage for her to ask the question, and it was a legitimate question to ask. She was just wrong in her evaluation of the situation. The format was not based on fear. People would accept the words better this way. I was sure of it.

"Hello, Russ Reed," I heard through static and the sounds of traffic in the distance.

"Hey Russ. It's me."

"Val, can you speak up. This connection sucks."

"Sure. Ruth read the proposal. She wrote me a letter."

"A letter?" Russ asked. "That's formal. What did she have to say?"

"Basically, that I'm not courageous."

"You're not courageous? That's what she said?" The static broke the line for a moment. "Val, Val, are you there?"

"Yeah, I'm here. Where are you?"

"Who knows, somewhere on the New Jersey Turnpike. It all looks the same. Now come on. Tell me what she really said. Read me the letter."

"That *is* what she really said," I answered, the anger biting in my mouth.

"Just read me the letter," Russ repeated. So I did.

"Val, she's not saying you're not courageous. She said lots of great things about the book. And you've got to give her credit for being honest."

"Just because she's being honest doesn't mean she's being right."

"Oookay," Russ said. "Look, Val. Ruth knows you're courageous. I know you're courageous. The whole damn federal government knows you're courageous. So just calm down a minute and—"

"Screw you. This isn't about fear. It's about strategy. I'm not afraid of the truth. I just decided—no, we decided. Don't you remember? We've had this conversation. We made this decision last year, for Christ's sake. Are you backing out now?"

"I'm not backing out of anything," Russ answered, his voice also rising. "Will you calm down? We should at least consider what she's saying. Maybe she has a point."

"You consider it," I hissed. "I've considered it already. I considered it last year." I was now turning all of my frustration toward Russ. "I discussed it with you then. We agreed."

"I know. I know we agreed. Get ahold of yourself. I'm just saying that maybe we should consider her point again."

"You don't have any idea what you're saying. Do you understand what that would mean? Do you? We would have to rewrite everything. The whole book would change."

"Look, I understand that—"

"You don't understand shit. I mean everything. Everything that I've done for the last year. Everything that I've done based on our agreement. That's what you want? That's what you're asking me to do?"

"Valerie, I'm not asking you to change anything. Would you listen to me? I just mean that we should think about what she is saying. You're right. We did discuss this. We did agree. I think we still do."

Russ stopped talking. I remained silent.

"Val, are you still there?" I still did not answer. "Oh no. Now I've really pissed her off," Russ added, laughing.

"I'm not afraid, Russ," I finally responded. "I'm not mad at Ruth either. It's great that she was honest. I know it would have been easier for her just to say 'looks great to me' and carry on. I do appreciate what she said. But I truly believe that she is wrong. I am not afraid—"

"Valerie, I know you're not afraid," Russ interjected.

"I'm not," I repeated. "If we tell the readers about us, they may focus on the messengers and not the message. If we tell them about Tahkamenon, they will either tune us out or, even worse, start looking for Tahkamenon themselves and fail to answer when Ralph or Mary comes knocking at their door."

"Do you think there's really a spirit named Ralph?" Russ asked.

"You know what I mean."

"I know. You're right." Russ's voice was gentle. "Are you okay?"

"I'm fine. I don't know why this upset me so much."

"Well, I do. It's been a tremendous amount of work. It's kind of late in the game to change everything now."

My anger started to rise. "I'm not concerned with the work," I shrieked. "I just don't think that she's right."

"Okay," Russ quickly responded. "That's what I meant. I mean we certainly don't want people turning away. And I think you're right about the Ralph thing. Everyone needs to find his or her own connection. That's what this is all about." We had to wait for a moment as static filled the line and then subsided.

"So we're still in agreement?" I asked when the line cleared.

"Yes, we're in agreement," Russ replied.

We talked for a few minutes longer and then said goodbye. I put Ruth's letter away in a file but could not shake her question from my mind. "Courage," I kept repeating to myself. "This has nothing to do with courage."

I called Ruth the next morning. She seemed relieved to hear from me. I thanked her for her insight and her honesty. I explained that Russ and I had considered the format and that we had agreed on a strategy of letting the message stand for itself. Later, after people had read some of the message, then we would tell them the story. We would explain our connection to each other. We would reveal our connection with Tahkamenon. I was calm and back in control. Ruth accepted my explanations easily. "There," I thought hanging up the phone with relief. "Now I can get back to the book."

But it wasn't that easy. Ruth's words kept ringing in my head. My reasoning was logical, but was it right? At first I tried not to ask. I did not tell Russ about my doubt. I did not want him to support her question. Or maybe I did not want him to support my reasoning. I was not certain which.

The whole issue seemed forgotten between us until several weeks later. Russ called me early one morning as I was working on the book. "Don't kill me," he started.

"What have you done now?" I asked, pulling myself from the tangle of words I had been wrestling with on my computer.

"I think maybe she's right."

"Maybe she is," I responded, needing no explanation of who "she" was. My tone was flat. I neither questioned him further on his thoughts nor provided any more insight into my own.

Russ was silent for a moment, obviously unsure which way to turn in the conversation. "I have my calendar in front of me," he eventually said. "How does next Wednesday look for you."

"That would be great. I really want to get together. I have so much to show you. I really need to reconnect."

"Yeah, me too," Russ responded. "Did I ever tell you how happy I am that we're doing this together?"

I smiled. He didn't need to say it. Even when we were fighting over one aspect of the book or another, I always knew. "Yeah, yeah," I replied. "Don't try to butter me up now. I am glad you're coming down, though." We confirmed the date, and I hurried off the phone. I wanted some quiet. I needed time to be alone with my thoughts.

I sat for several hours, thinking of everything that had transpired. It was almost impossible to remember my life before Tahkamenon. It was so distant, and in retrospect, everything seemed to lead to this moment. I remembered a sentence that I had read many years before: "So this is the point to where my life has taken me." The moment swelled with potential and the statement reverberated in my mind. It was both authentic and appropriate. This was the point to where my life had brought me. And it was up to me to choose the next step.

I thought again of Ruth's words. I truly appreciated her sincerity. But she was wrong. The format was not about fear. It was a decision, a question of timing, a matter of strategy. It was—

My thoughts faltered, and all of the rationalization of the last year unraveled at my feet. In their void, I heard the gentle whispers of my soul, whispers that spoke to me clearly, without judgment, without fear. It *was* about courage. It had all been about courage. Not the courage it takes to believe in Tahkamenon but the courage it takes to believe in ourselves.

My heart swelled with the inspiration of Tahkamenon's words. I thought of Russ, of the beauty of our connection, of the blessing of our mutual discovery. I wanted to call him, but the call had to wait.

My being was engulfed by the words that had emerged from the depths of our souls, forever woven into the tapestry of our lives:

Choose love. You are divine, your soul protected. There are individual realities and mass realities. This is the voice of peace you have heard forever. You not only hear the song but also add to it. I love you. You are as my child and my friend. You are both a piece of the puzzle and the universal picture the puzzle strives to represent. Both instrument and symphony. Trust this. Have faith.

This is a gift that grows with the giving, magnified and reinforced by each heart that it touches, by each soul that finds a ray of light. The gift I bring lies waiting within your soul. I come only to open the door. No future day will be as loveless as the past. It is not upon you to create perfection; it is your destiny to accept it. Do not be deceived by the simplicity of these words. They break the barriers of many lifetimes and vibrate with an eternity of light.

Remember always, this is a great journey upon which we embark.

Silently I thanked Tahkamenon, my soul pulsing with the gentle vibrations of his light. I remembered a commitment I had made months ago—words that follow my heart as closely as my ability allows.

I understood what Ruth was saying. We could not effectively tell the message without having the courage to tell our story. It was the spiritual and the physical all wrapped into one. It was the only way that the words could resonate with our being. It was the only way that we could fully confront our fears.

I now knew without question what it was that Tahkamenon wanted. So I picked up my pen and allowed my heart to sing:

"I never considered entertaining spirits . . ."

The End
(and also The Beginning)

Epilogue

It is the beginning, always the beginning. If Tahkamenon has taught us anything, it's the continual nature of our journey. We hope that we keep moving closer.
But sometimes not. And in those times we have to remember to halt the movement and listen.

Russ and I hope that, as you've read our story and the
passages of our connection, you have experienced your
own. That you have felt glimmers of recognition and moments of light. That you have heard the whispering not of
our souls but of yours. And that you find the courage to
act in accordance with your heart.

You carry divinity, perfection, and love within you.
You know the truth. You understand the light. Your ability is endless. Your beauty untold. And all are at your
disposal if only you choose to reconnect with your soul.

The world does not constrain you. Your walls do not
constrain you. Only your fear can withhold you and then
only with your permission and lack of faith.

We wish you well on your journey and look forward to
that moment when we will meet again.

About the Authors

Valerie Wilkinson

Growing up in a trailer in the mountains of rural Pennsylvania, Ms. Wilkinson learned a great deal about the exclusion of those with little money or demographic significance. She moved on from those beginnings to graduate with highest honors from Penn State University, pass the CPA exam, run a multi-million dollar health care company, and relate both as friend and foe with the Washington power brokers, politicians, and government officials.

Ms. Wilkinson resides in Virginia Beach, Virginia, with her husband, Brian, and their three young children, Ashleigh, Eric, and Alex. She has written speeches for both state and national politicians and ghostwrites communications for business leaders, regional and international charities, and political figures on a wide array of topics directed at diverse audiences. It remains her goal to contribute to the enrichment of humanity and inspire others to do the same.

Russell Reed

In 1970, Mr. Reed had recently returned from Vietnam, graduated from Lafayette College, and began a career in the field of employee benefits, working for the Hartford Insurance Company. In 1980, he moved to New York City, advancing his career throughout the 80s, becoming a vice-president and achieving all the trappings of success. In 1990, he left his employer of twenty years and started his own business. As the millennium approaches, Mr. Reed is a successful entrepreneur. He is totally committed to reaching out to others and spreading the powerful message of peace found in *Whispers from Our Soul, The Voice of Tahkamenon.*

Mr. Reed lives in Buckingham, Pennsylvania, with his wife Mary Ellen and their daughter Autumn. He has a married son, Peter, who lives in Atlanta.

The authors met through business, developing a unique connection and joint desire to give voice to the songs of their hearts.